TILDA'S TOY BOX

Tone Finnanger

D&C

David and Charles

www.ilovetilda.com

Foreword

Tilda's Toy Box has been a wonderful book to create from beginning to end thanks to the excellent help from all the designers and photographers, but also because of the gorgeous projects and the opportunity to immerse myself in the world of children. It was lovely to have a good excuse to play!

This book is entirely devoted to projects that you can sew for children, and we've made sure that all the toys are functional; you can take the clothes on and off them and they will withstand a lot of wear and tear.

I'm extremely grateful for the fabulous input from the clever ladies who took part in producing the book: Ingunn Eløy, who sewed almost all the projects following my explanations and patterns; Ingrid Skansaar, who helped with the scenes and styled and organised the photoshoots; Sølvi Dos Santos, who brought life to the photos; and Emma, our beautiful, charismatic model. The quilting projects were assembled and quilted with Crazy Pussle by Lappelises Quiltestue in Sandefjord.

Many thanks also go to the publisher, Cappelen Damm, who give me a lot of freedom and support in producing my books, and to David & Charles, who take the books out into the big, wide world with such enthusiasm.

And last, but not least, my family, who took it in their stride when the house was turned upside down during photoshoots and who were there for me when needed.

 I really hope you find something you enjoy making!

Kindest regards,

Tone Finnanger

contents

DOLLS

♥ 12

SEA and WATER
♥ 68

EXOTIC ANIMALS
♥ 90

patterns 120

Safety

A manufactured toy is tested extensively before it can be put on sale but when you sew one yourself you must ensure it is safe. Please bear in mind the following when sewing for children.

SMALL PARTS

The toys in this book are not recommended for small children who put things in their mouths. Many of the toys have small parts that can become loose, and buttons that can look like sweets to young children.

ELASTICS AND HAIRBANDS

Pay special attention to any elastic and hairbands: these could be a choking hazard if a child puts these around their neck.

ALLERGIES

Children can be allergic to some materials, so choose with care. Always wash fabrics before sewing them for children, as some fabrics can contain allergenic chemicals.

HIDDEN PINS

When sewing for children, it is extremely important not to leave pins or needles in the toy. Always check thoroughly.

Wear and tear

A toy will be as resistant to wear and tear as you make it. To make a more hard-wearing toy, sew double seams and fasten arms and legs with embroidery thread. It is especially important to fasten loose parts securely, such as tufts of hair, buttons and bows on hairbands.

Materials

The toys in this book are all made from washed Tilda cotton fabrics. The range also contains plain cotton, suitable for dolls' skin. We use synthetic filling, which is non-allergenic.

Hair and eyes for the dolls and animals are painted using Palett textile paint for light fabrics, obtainable from Panduro Hobby. This is a non-toxic textile paint that has been heat-tempered to withstand washing.

Rouge is applied with the stamp pad included in the Tilda Face Painting Kit, part 71340. It is child-friendly, non-toxic and water-soluble.

Instructions for making the hair and eyes can be found in Faces and Hair.

Washing

Stuffed toys, such as dolls and monkeys, are not suitable for washing as the filling can move about or become uneven. If you have to wash a toy, we recommend wiping it with a cloth. Try not to allow the toy to become soaked through.

Tilda rouge is water-soluble and can easily be re-applied. Dolls' clothes can be washed carefully on a hand wash at 40 degrees. Machine-sewn patchwork quilts and cushions can be washed in a washing machine on a 40-degree programme.

Faces and hair

The positioning of the hair and eyes makes a big difference to the toy's appearance. It is a good idea to use a pen with vanishing ink or an air-erasable pen when outlining the hair. If you can't get hold of one, you could carefully use a pencil or faint pen.

LARGE DOLL

Measure 6cm (2¼in) down from the seam at the top of the head and insert a pin as the starting point for where the curve of the fringe meets the seam in the face. Outline the hair as shown in figure A and the photos of the dolls.

To position the eyes, measure 11cm (4¼in) down from the seam at the top of the head following the seam in the middle of the face. Insert a pin. Next measure 4cm (1½in) either side and insert pins to mark the position of the eyes, so there is 8cm (3¼in) between them, see figure A. Use your judgement a little, as there will always be some movement and variation when you sew, however, we found that this formula worked on all the dolls we tested.

The simplest way to apply eyes is to use a pin with a large rounded head, such as the largest headed pin in Tilda pins, part 480933. Twist the pin backwards and forwards to make a visible hole to mark where the eye is to be positioned. Dip the pinhead in the Palett textile paint and use it to stamp eyes onto the figure.

If you don't have a pin of this type, you can either find something else to stamp with, or draw an even circle with a diameter of approximately 7mm (¼in) around the hole and paint the eyes with a thin paintbrush. Dry the eyes with a hairdryer.

SMALL DOLL

First measure 3.4cm (1⅜in) down to the hairline, then measure a further 6cm (2¼in) down to determine where the eyes are to be placed, see figure B. There should be 4.2cm (1½in) space between the eyes.

Make the eyes in the same way as for the Large Doll, using a normal large-headed pin, so you have a diameter of 3–4mm (⅛–³⁄₁₆in).

DOLL'S HAIR

Paint an edge that follows the outline of the hair, making sure your lines are sharp and even. On the back of the head, the hair can be outlined in a gentle curve from side to side.

Paint the area inside the edge, including the tufts of hair, see figure C. Dry the paint with a hairdryer. The heat hardens the textile paint.

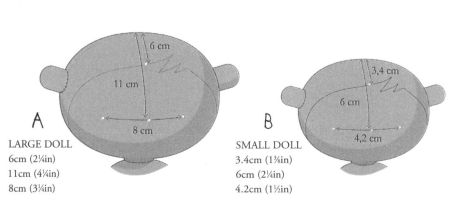

A

LARGE DOLL
6cm (2¼in)
11cm (4¼in)
8cm (3¼in)

B

SMALL DOLL
3.4cm (1⅜in)
6cm (2¼in)
4.2cm (1½in)

C

MONKEYS

The monkey's eyes are similar to the large doll's, but they can be placed wherever you wish. The same applies to the eyes for the appliqué monkey on the Monkey Cushion. Look at the photos of the monkeys and use pins to try out different positions.

OTHER ANIMALS

Parrots, snakes and large whales have eyes similar to the large doll, whereas small whales are similar to the small doll. Refer to the photos to help you to position the eyes.

ROUGE

Rouge or lipstick is only applied to the cheeks of figures with skin-coloured faces, i.e. dolls and monkeys. Faces made from patterned fabric look better without rouge.

The Tilda face kit, part 713400, contains a rouge stamp pad, which is child-friendly and non-toxic. Alternatively, you can use a small amount of lipstick. Brush the colour on with a dry paintbrush.

patchwork and quilting

Here you can find tips and advice on how to make the patchwork items included in the book, such as quilts and cushions.

EQUIPMENT

When you cut out materials for patchworking, it is useful if you have patchwork-cutting tools, obtainable from quilting shops. These include a cutting mat, patchwork rulers (available in various sizes) and a roller knife with a rounded blade.

We recommend getting hold of these tools and some basic knowledge before starting to make the patchwork projects. You can find the information you need from quilting shops or by searching on the Internet.

MEASUREMENTS

The most common measuring unit for patchwork and quilting is the inch, which is equivalent to 2.54cm. It's usually rounded off to 2.5cm to make measurements simpler.

There are many advantages to using inches. Measurements on rulers and instructions often give measurements in inches, and round numbers are often quite complicated to convert into centimetres. 10 inches can be written as 10" or 10in and next to the inch measurement is the cm measurement in brackets, for example: 3½in (8.75cm).

We have written the patchwork and quilting measurements throughout the book as inches first followed by centimetres. Other measurements throughout the book are written in the usual way: centimetres first, followed by inches in brackets, so you can work with the measuring unit that you prefer.

SEAM ALLOWANCES

Seam allowances have to be added to patterns in the book unless the instructions say otherwise. You need to add a seam allowance of 6mm (¼in) unless otherwise stated.

Seam allowances are already included in the size specifications for the patchwork projects to make things easier. Seam allowances are calculated at 6mm (¼in).

WADDING AND BACK PIECES

When you have finished a patch, whether it's for a quilt or a cushion, a piece of quilting wadding (batting) is mounted to the back of the front piece and then a layer of fabric is added to the back piece before it is quilted. We use cotton wadding.

There are many techniques for sewing the layers together while you are quilting: safety pins, a quilt basting gun or large tack (basting) stitches. The simplest method is perhaps to use a basting spray.

QUILTING

There are many quilting techniques, from simple straightforward seams to intricate seams that require knowledge and experience. You can find out more about quilting methods in quilting shops and on the Internet.

BINDING

Cut 6cm (2¼in) wide strips for the binding, seam allowance is included. Join the strips together until you have a strip long enough to bind all the edges.

Iron the binding strip in half, wrong sides together, so it measures 3cm (1¼in) wide.

Place one side of the folded strip over the edge of the quilt or cushion and sew in one seam allowance, see figure A.

At each corner, stop approximately one seam allowance from the edge. Fold the edge so you have a neat fold in the corner before continuing to sew, see figure B.

When you have sewn one side of the binding in place around the whole of the quilt, fold it over the edge and sew the other side in place on the back, see figure C.

A

B

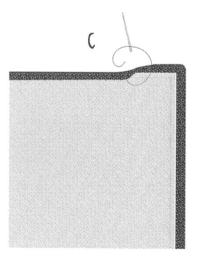

C

DOLLS

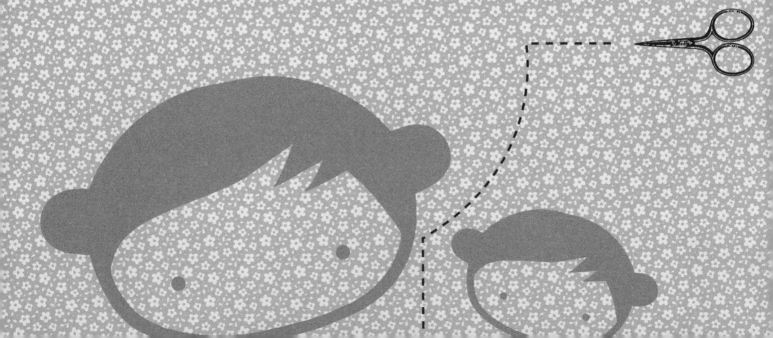

"Dolls aren't born with a name. When you see a doll for the first time, you will know what it should be called."

Doll's body

You can find the templates in the Patterns *section.*

All the dolls in the book have tufts of hair, quite simply because we think they're so sweet, but they can easily be left out if you prefer. The doll works just as well as a girl or boy.

GETTING STARTED

HEAD

Fold the two head parts away from each other, place right sides facing and sew around, see figure A. Sew double seams and leave the neck opening unsewn, see figure B.

Trim off the extra seam allowance around the edge, remembering to cut nicks where the seam allowance curves in. Turn the head right side out and iron.

To give the head a good shape, it must be stuffed well. Start by pushing the stuffing towards the outer edges and keep filling until the head is full. Then push in more stuffing towards the face and back of the head to achieve a good round shape. Don't be afraid of kneading and shaping the head, but be careful that the seams don't split under excess pressure.

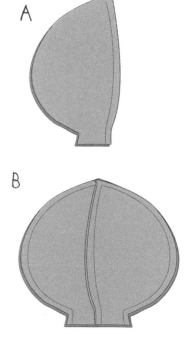

A

B

YOU WILL NEED

Skin fabric
Wool stuffing
Tools for hair and face,
see Faces and Hair

BODY

Fold the fabric for the body in half, right sides facing, and transfer the pattern of the body, two arms, two legs and two tufts of hair.

Mark the openings and sew around the parts. Cut out, remembering to cut nicks in the seam allowance where the seam curves in. Turn the parts right side out and iron.

To turn thin legs and arms right side out, push the blunt end of a wooden stick towards the tip of the arm/leg, see figure C. Begin at the foot/hand and pull the leg/arm down over the wooden stick, see figure D. Hold onto the foot/hand and pull downwards while holding on, so that the leg/arm is turned right side out, see figure E.

Stuff the legs, arms and tufts of hair using the wooden stick. Stuff the body. Position the legs on the body and fasten them with pins, then sew up the opening of the body to secure the legs in place, see figure F. Remove pins.

Fold in the seam allowance around the opening on the head, stuff it well and sew the head in place. Attach the head very close to the body: there should only be a couple of millimetres of neck showing.

Fasten the arms to the body. So that they have lots of movement make the fastening point small, but strong. To do this, sew a small area of the arm securely onto the body using a lot of stitches or embroidery thread, see figure G.

Fold in the seam allowance around the opening to the tufts of hair. Fasten them with pins, using the photograph as a reference. They must be fastened on the reverse of the side seam, slightly up from the middle of each side of the head. Sew securely in place.

Paint the hair and face, see Faces and Hair.

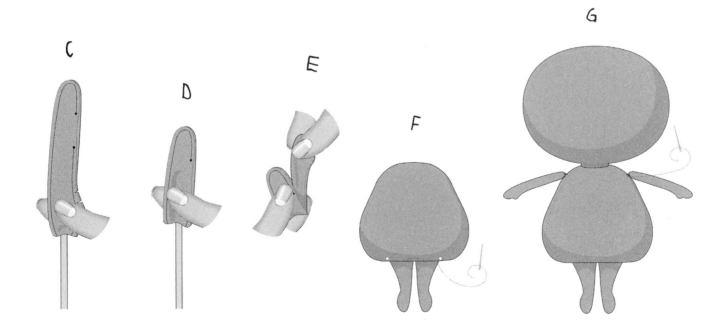

knickers and trousers

You can find the templates in the Patterns *section.*

Knickers and trousers are sewn in the same way, although the knickers are shorter in the legs than the trousers. We used flat elastic for the trousers and round hat elastic for the knickers. Flat elastic gives a more secure edge, which is ideal for trousers, whereas the round elastic is thinner and suits knickers better.

GETTING STARTED

Cut out the four parts for the knickers/trousers, making sure that you draw a channel for the elastic in the waist and leg openings, as well as an extra seam allowance.

Place two pairs of parts right sides facing and sew together along the side of the knickers/trousers, see figure A.

Fold the knicker/trouser parts away from each other and sew the curves together on each side, see figure B.

A
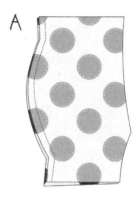

B
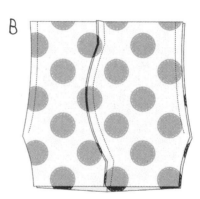

YOU WILL
NEED

Fabric
Flat elastic or round
hat elastic

Fold the knickers/trousers the opposite way so that the seams lie above and below each other. Sew up the legs, see figure C.

Fold the seam allowance at the waist opening, and then fold over to create the channel for the elastic. Sew along the folded edge of the seam allowance. Keep a 2cm (¾in) opening so that you can thread the elastic through later.

Do the same on each leg, see figure D. For the trouser legs, it is easier to sew the edge in place by hand.

Cut off ample lengths of elastic: you will need enough for the circumference of the openings, plus a little extra. Thread the elastic through the waist and leg channels, either by using a safety pin, or attaching some thread to the elastic and pulling it through the channels using a blunt needle, see figure E.

Pull the knickers/trousers onto the doll and tighten the elastic to fit. If you use hat elastic, tie a knot and cut off the ends. If you use flat elastic, note which of the two ends should be fastened together.

Take the trousers off the figure, tighten the elastic and fasten the ends together with a pin. Sew backwards and forwards to fasten the ends of the elastic together, using a sewing machine if preferred. Cut off any excess elastic.

Sew up the openings used to thread the elastic through the waist and on each leg.

Turn the knickers/trousers right side out, iron and put them on the doll.

C

D

E

Apron dress

You can find the templates in the Patterns *section.*

GETTING STARTED

The bodice is comprised of three parts and must be lined. The easiest method is to line it using the same fabric that is used for the dress itself. Cut out two of each of the dress parts, including a good seam allowance; you should have six parts altogether. Remember that you need a right and left side part for both the fabric and lining, see figure A.

Sew the two side parts securely to the middle section, so you have two identical bodices. Place the bodices right sides facing and sew together. Do not sew along the bottom edge, see figure B. Cut off the excess seam allowance, turn the bodice right side out, then iron.

A

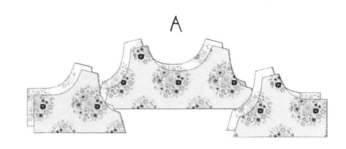

B

Cut a strip measuring 52 x 6.5cm (20 x 25½in) for the skirt. One long side and each short side should be folded in twice to hide the unsewn edge, so add an ample seam allowance. The other long side should have a normal seam allowance.

Fold the three above-mentioned sides in twice, iron and sew to hold the fold in place.

Use a sewing machine to sew approximately 6mm (¼in) long stitches along the last long side (waist) and pull the bottom thread tight to gather up the edge.

Pull and adjust the gathered waist edge so that it is the same length as the bodice, and spread the gathers as evenly as you can.

Place the right side of the bodice on the waist edge of the skirt, so that the edges lie against each other and sew the skirt in place, see figure C.

Sew a zigzag seam outside the fastening seam.

For the best results, fasten the dress at the back using a press-stud. Put the dress on the doll and mark where each half of the press-stud should be placed before sewing them in position, see figure D.

C

D

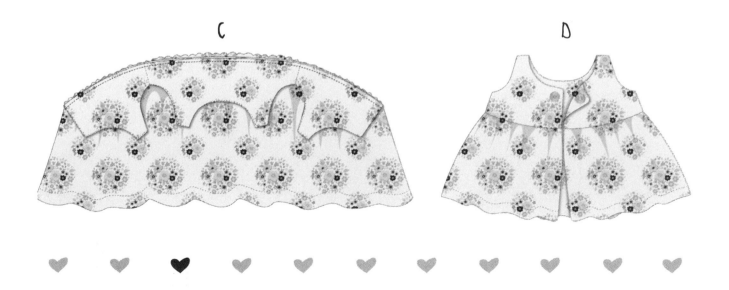

jacket

You can find the templates in the *Patterns* section.

GETTING STARTED

The jacket is lined, but we have not lined the sleeves, as this would make them too stiff. Cut out the three parts for the jacket from the jacket fabric and the jacket lining. Also, cut out two sleeves from the jacket fabric, but not from the lining, see figure A. Allow for plenty of seam allowance on all parts.

Mark out the darts carefully, following the pattern. The arrows on the pattern show the direction that the middle of the dart should lie, see figure B. Fold the darts in the same way as the jacket parts and lining parts.

Iron the darts well and sew a small seam across each dart to secure it. The seam should be in the seam allowance, so that it isn't visible on the finished jacket, see figure C.

Fold the fabric for the two collar parts in half, right sides facing, sew around and cut out. Turn right side out and iron.

Sew the three jacket fabric and lining parts together at the shoulders. Sew the sleeves in place on the jacket part, see figure D.

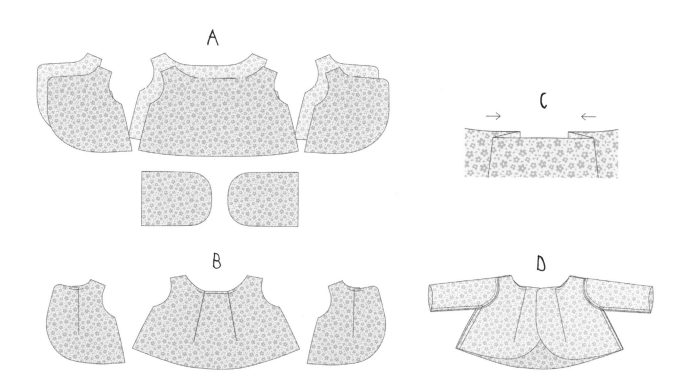

A

C

B

D

Place the front jacket part right sides facing on the back jacket part. Pin the jacket and lining together all around the edge. Make sure the sleeves aren't in the way and sew around the whole of the jacket, see figure E. Leave a reverse opening in the middle of the back of the jacket, see figure F.

It's very important to cut off the excess seam allowance along the edge. Cut nicks in the seam allowance under the sleeves and where the seams curve in to avoid stretching. Fold the seam allowance in at the opening to each sleeve twice, so the unsewn edge is hidden, and sew in place by hand. The stitches should not go through the fabric. Turn the jacket right side out and iron well.

So that the lining is not too loose in the jacket, we have folded in the seam allowance at the sleeve openings in the lining and sewn in place in the seam allowance where the sleeves are fastened on the jacket, see figure G.

Put the jacket on the doll and work out where to place the hook and loop fastening, so that the jacket can be done up easily. Cut out and sew the hook and loop fastening parts in place. Sew a button on the front on the side that overlaps the hook and loop fastening when the jacket is done up, see figure H. For older children, you can sew buttonholes and fasten with buttons in the usual way.

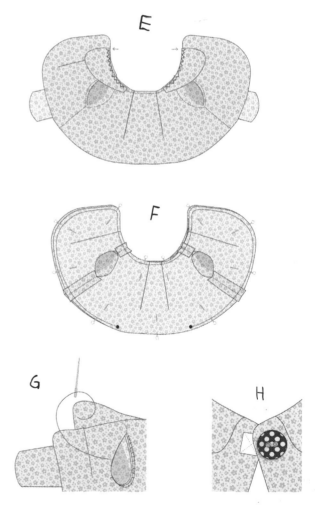

Hair accessories

You can find the templates in the Patterns *section.*

It's fun being able to swap between different adornments. Here you can make all sorts of hairbands and hair elastics.

GETTING STARTED

HAIRBAND

Cut out a strip of fabric measuring 32 x 5.5cm (12½ x 2¼in) for the hairband, adding a seam allowance.

Fold the strip in half, right sides facing, so that it measures 2.75cm (1⅛in) wide, and sew up the open long side. Turn the strip right side out, fold in the seam allowance at the opening on each end and iron.

Cut another strip measuring 14 x 4cm (5½ x 1½in) to cover the elastic. Sew it in the same way as the hairband, so it is 2cm (¾in) wide. Don't fold in the seam allowances on either side.

Cut a strip of elastic measuring 8cm (3¼in). Thread the elastic into the thin strip with the elastic and fabric aligning at one end. Fasten these two ends together by sewing backwards and forwards with a sewing machine. Pull the other end of the elastic through the fabric so that you can fasten the other ends together.

Thread one end of the covered elastic through the hairband. Sew one end of the elastic in place and sew up the opening, see figure A.

Thread the other end of the covered elastic into the other end of the hairband. Fasten with a pin, see figure B.

Fold the fabric for the bow in half, right sides facing, transfer the pattern for the bow and sew around, then cut out and turn right side out. Iron the bow and sew up the reverse opening.

Tie a single knot in the middle of the bow. Put the hairband on the doll and position the bow using a pin, before sewing it in place, see figure C. Remove all pins.

HAIR ELASTIC

Measure a piece of flat elastic around the tuft of hair on the doll's head and mark where the elastic is to be sewn together to hold it in place. Cut out a piece of elastic slightly longer than the marks.

Cut a fabric strip measuring 14 x 4cm (5½ x 1½in) to cover the elastic. Sew it in the same way as the hairband, so it is a 2cm (¾in) wide tube. Fold in the seam allowance at both ends and thread the elastic through the tube. Fasten the ends of the elastic together with a pin, just inside the marks, and sew together by sewing backwards and forwards, preferably with a sewing machine. Remove all pins.

Cut off the excess elastic and sew the tube openings together so the fabric strip covers the elastic.

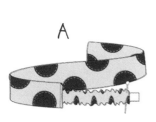

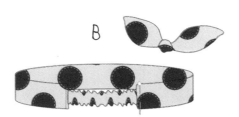

YOU WILL NEED

Fabric
Flat elastic

Decorations

You can find the templates in the Patterns *section.*

The rosette and flower decorations are sewn in the same way. The rosette is lovely for the jacket and dress, and the flower suits most accessories. It is important to avoid the thickest type of interfacing, as it's almost impossible to sew through several layers.

GETTING STARTED

Iron your chosen fabrics against the adhesive side of the interfacing and transfer the pattern onto the rosette or flower parts on the fabric side.

Use a sewing machine to stitch approximately 6mm (¼in) in from the outlined edge. Cut out the parts according to the outlined edge, see figure A.

Place the parts on top of one another with a button on the top. Sew the button in place through all the layers so they are all sewn together at the same time.

Tip: If you sew a piece of hook and loop fastening onto the jacket or dress and then sew the other part of the hook and loop fastening to the back of a flower and rosette, you will be able to change the decoration on the jacket or dress.

A

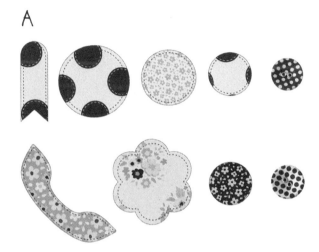

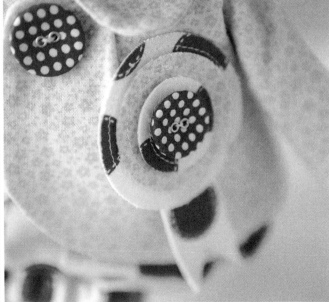

YOU WILL NEED

Fabrics
Interfacing for bags with an
adhesive side
A button
An air erasable pen is
recommended

Doll's doll

You can find the templates in the Patterns *section.*

The small doll is sewn in the same way as the large doll, except the body and legs are sewn as one piece and the arms are slightly simpler. You will need a small wooden stick, such as a plant stick, preferably with a point, for turning the small arms and tufts of hair right side out.

GETTING STARTED

Cut out the parts for the head, place right sides facing and sew. Turn right sides out and stuff the head in the same way as for the large doll.

Fold the fabric for the body, arms and tufts of hair, right sides facing, and transfer the pattern onto the fabric. Note that the arms have a reverse opening at the end and not in the seam like the large doll. Cut out, turn right side out and iron.

Stuff the parts, using the wooden stick to help you, and sew up the reverse opening on the body. Sew the head and tufts of hair in place in the same way as for the large doll. Fold in the seam allowance at the opening of the arms and sew them in place on the doll, see figure A.

Paint the hair and complete the face, see Faces and Hair.

A

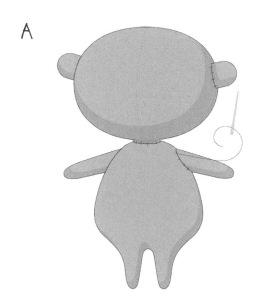

YOU WILL NEED

Skin fabric
Wool stuffing
Tools for hair and face, see
Faces and Hair

Small knickers

You can find the templates in the Patterns *section.*

The best idea for tiny knickers is to sew them as a kind of tube, then sew together the centre of the bottom edge to form two holes for the legs.

GETTING STARTED

Cut out the two parts for the knickers, then calculate the seam allowance and channel for the elastic, as shown in the pattern. Place the pieces right sides facing and sew together on each side.

Fold in the seam allowance and fold the fabric over to form a channel for the elastic at both edges. Sew around the edges on the outside of the fold. Leave an opening to thread the elastic through, see figure A.

Thread in the elastic with a very small safety pin or by threading the elastic into a short, blunt needle. You can also use a piece of steel wire with a loop at the front and back.

Put the knickers on the doll and tie the elastic to fit so it is fairly tight. Don't tighten the elastic too much at the leg opening otherwise it won't look like two legs when you finish.

Sew up the channels for the elastic. Sew the middle of the leg opening to form two holes for the doll's legs, see figure B.

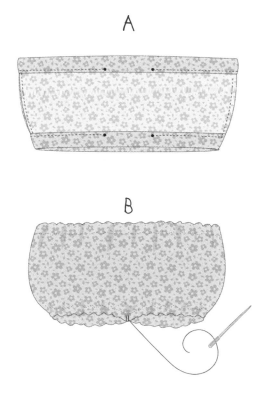

A

B

Small dress

You can find the templates in the Patterns *section.*

Although it is fiddly, it looks best if you fold in the seam allowance around the dress twice so the unsewn edge is hidden. Alternatively, you can sew a zigzag seam around the edge and then fold it in just once.

GETTING STARTED

Cut out the three parts for the dress, making sure you have two opposite side parts. Fold in and sew all the edges, apart from the short sides under the diagonals for the arms where the dress parts are to be sewn together.

Place the two side parts on the middle section, right sides facing, and sew together along the short sides, see figure A.

Mark the two darts in the middle section and sew them in at the top by hand. Next, sew the shoulders together by hand, see figure B.

Put the dress on the small doll and mark where the press-stud is to be attached before sewing it in place.

YOU WILL NEED

Fabric for the dress
A press-stud

YOU WILL NEED

Various pieces of fabric
Interfacing for bags
Cotton wadding (batting)
Zip
Paper piecing glue or quick-drying
hobby glue
A button
Optional: quilting spray adhesive

Handbag house

You can find the templates in the Patterns *section.*

The handbag house is designed to be a mobile house for the small doll who, thanks to her size, is the perfect travel companion. The idea behind the bag is simple; you sew and edge four stiff walls, a floor and a soft, padded roof with a zip, then you sew the parts together at the edges to construct a house. This project requires a lot of work, so the instructions are lengthy, but the result is well worth the effort.

GETTING STARTED

STIFF WALLS AND FLOOR

The walls and floor are stiffened by adding a layer of strong interfacing for bags to the middle, along with two layers of wadding (batting) – one on each side of the interfacing – and fabric for a soft, quilted surface that is easy to sew on.

Cut out two house shapes, two side walls and a floor from the thick interfacing. Then cut four house shapes, four side walls and two floors from the cotton wadding and the same from the fabric.

If you want a different fabric for the lining, cut out two house shapes, two side walls and a floor from both the main fabric and the fabric for the lining. Add a seam allowance for all parts (this will be cut off later in the process).

It is a good idea to use quilting spray adhesive when fastening the layers together, but it will work without it just as well.

Place or glue a layer of wadding on each side of the interfacing to make a sandwich, then place the fabric on one side and lining fabric on the other side of the sandwich. The right sides of the fabrics must be facing outwards on both sides, see figure A.

Make sure that all layers are aligned exactly and press the layers together with an iron. Sew the layers together around the edge.

The parts for the house are quilted with straight, horizontal seams, as drawn on the pattern. Measure up the seams, following the pattern, and make a mark at the top and bottom so you know where to sew.

Sew all the quilting seams. Carefully transfer the pattern again and cut off all the seam allowance. Sew a zigzag seam around the edge of each of the parts, see figure B.

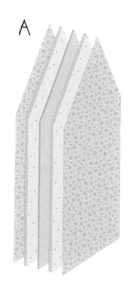

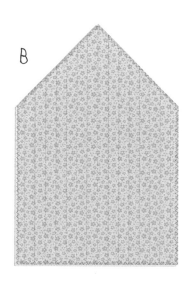

APPLIQUÉS

Only the front and one side wall are appliquéd, as shown in the photograph. Interfacing for bags is used to make the appliqués stand out from the house. The easiest way to fasten the fabric around the interfaced appliqués is to apply glue around the edges. It is best to use a glue pen for paper piecing and appliqués, but since this is a model that shouldn't be washed you can also use quick-drying hobby glue.

Cut out the door, window, sign, small heart, bird and the shapes for the two potted trees from the strong interfacing used for the walls. Do not include any seam allowance, simply cut carefully along the pattern line.

DOOR AND WINDOW

Cut out a window section from your chosen fabric and fasten it to the interfacing by applying a little glue along the edges. Repeat with your chosen fabric for the door.

Sew a cross on the window, as drawn on the pattern, using a thick zigzag seam approximately 3mm (⅛in) wide.

Bind the edges of the door and window with 2cm (¾in) wide fabric strips. Don't fold the strips in half as you would when edging a quilt, but leave them as a single layer.

Place a strip the same width as the door, right sides facing, along the edge at the top of the door and sew in place approximately 4mm (⅛in) in, see figure C. Iron the strip upwards and fold it around the edge of the door, fastening it on the back with glue.

Cut out two strips approximately 1cm (⅜in) taller than the door. Place right sides facing and sew in place on each side, approximately 4mm (⅛in) in, see figure D.

Iron the strips outwards on each side. Now fold the extra 1cm (⅜in) around the top on each side and glue in place, see figure E. Then fold each long side around the edge and glue in place, see figure F. For neat corners, it is a good idea to cut off any excess fabric at the corners. The edge at the bottom of the door will be hidden later by the edge around the house.

Bind the window edges in the same way, but first sew on a strip at the top and bottom. You will need to add 2cm (¾in) to the height of the window when fitting the side strips, so you have enough to fold in on the underside of the window.

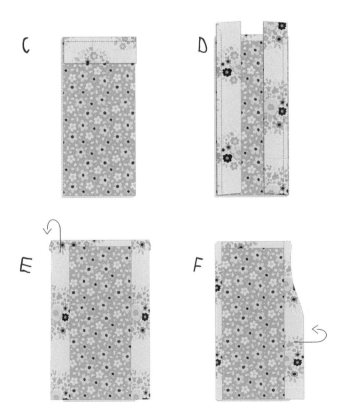

SIGN AND APPLIQUÉ PARTS

If the curly writing on the sign is too difficult, you can use simple stitches to add a name.

Cut out a piece of off-white fabric for the sign, adding approximately 1cm (⅜in) seam allowance around the edge. Transfer the wording onto the fabric using a faint pencil line or an air erasable pen. Stitch the writing using red thread, see figure G.

Place the stitched piece of fabric onto the interfaced sign and glue the seam allowance around the edge. Sew around the edge, see figure H.

Cut out the fabric for the other appliqué shapes: crown of tree, pot, leaf, small heart for the door and bird. Decide which parts of the fabric patterns you want on the front of the shapes when cutting them out.

Allow plenty of seam allowance for gluing around the edges of the interfacing shapes. The seam allowance for the small leaf must be small and is trimmed off once you have glued it around the edge.

For the heart shape, cut nicks in the seam allowance where the part curves in and out, so the fabric is pulled nicely around the edge, see figure I.

As with the bottom edge of the door, the bottom of the pot will be hidden later under the binding around the house, so you don't need to fold in the seam allowance here. Cut it off at the edge with the bottom of the pot, see figure J.

The tree trunk in the pot is made without interfacing, by cutting a narrow strip of fabric, approximately 8mm (⅜in) wide. Apply glue to the reverse side and fold/roll in a thin edge on one side. Apply a little more glue and fold in the other side to form a very thin trunk.

When you are happy with the positioning of the shapes on the house fasten them in place with a little glue then sew them in place. Sew a small beak on the bird with red sewing thread.

WAVY EDGE

A wavy edge is attached to the top of each side wall as a decoration.

Fold the fabric for the wavy edges right sides facing, transfer the pattern and sew. Only the wavy edge needs to be sewn; the sides and top will be hidden under the binding around the wall. Cut out the wavy edges and cut nicks where the seam curves in. Allow for a seam allowance at the open sides.

Turn the wavy edges right side out using a wooden stick then iron. Place the pattern on the sewn wavy edge and carefully cut off the seam allowance along the pattern line. Place a wavy edge at the top of each side wall and sew in place with a zigzag seam along the top edge and the two short sides.

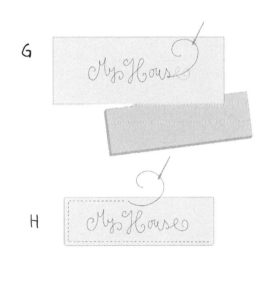

ROOF

The roof is sewn with a layer of wadding (batting). Cut out two roof halves from the fabric for the inside and two for the outside of the roof, as well as two wadding (batting) parts. Add seam allowance.

Attach the wadding to the wrong side of the fabric shapes for the outside of the roof, using either quilting spray adhesive or by sewing a zigzag seam around the edge.

Place the padded roof shape on the edge of the front of the zip right sides facing, and the fabric shape on the edge of the back of the zip right sides facing. Sew up the edges, see figure K. Iron the shapes outwards, see figure L.

Sew the other roof shapes in place on the opposite side of the zip.

Mark the quilting seams according to the pattern and quilt the roof. Place the pattern on top and cut off the seam allowance. The ends of the zip must also be cut.

BINDING

All the parts for the house have binding in the same way as a quilt, but with a thinner edge than usual.

Cut out 3.5cm (1⅜in) wide strips. Make sure you have enough strips and they are good length to bind all the house shapes. Avoid having a join for a more professional finish.

Iron the strips in half so they are 1.75cm (1¾in) wide. Place a strip edge to edge with one of the house shapes and sew approximately 4mm (⅛in) in from the edge.

At each corner, stop approximately 5mm (¼in) from the edge and make a neat fold in the corner before continuing to sew, see figure M. The angle at the bottom of the house is gradual so you can sew the binding in place as normal without having to make a fold.

When you have sewn the binding in place around one side, fold it tightly over to the other side and sew in place. Continue until all the house shapes have binding.

K   L

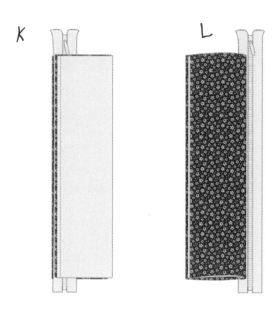

M

ASSEMBLY

Join the walls together by sewing along the edges to form the house shape, see the photograph of the house. It is easy to adjust the walls if they vary slightly in size. A little crookedness can also be quite charming.

Finish by sewing the roof in place. It is a good idea to tack (baste) the centre of the roof against the top of the house first, then straighten and tack (baste) each side of the short walls. This will ensure the roof fits and is in the right place before you sew along the edges.

We used a straight needle when sewing the house together, although using a curved needle in difficult areas may have made the task easier.

SHOULDER STRAP

Cut out a strip of fabric measuring 85 x 7cm (33½ x 2¾in) for the handbag strap and an 83 x 5cm (32½ x 2in) strip of cotton wadding (batting), seam allowance is included.

Place the wadding strip in the middle of the wrong side of the fabric strip. Fold and iron the edges of the fabric in over the top of the wadding. Fold the strip in half so it is approximately 2.5cm (1in) wide and sew approximately 5mm (¼in) in along all the sides.

Fasten the strip by sewing on a button with embroidery thread through both the wall and the strip on each side of the house. You need to sew several stitches to hold the button firmly in place, so it would be a good idea to use pliers or scissors to make it easier to pull the needle through all the layers.

sewing kit house

You can find the templates in the Patterns *section.*

This charming sewing kit is not suitable for small children, but it's great for older children that are just learning to sew or for adults to store all their sewing sundries.

GETTING STARTED

The sewing kit is made from two house-shaped walls, similar to those on the Handbag House, only smaller. There are two things to note that are different from the walls on the Handbag House: there's a pocket on the inside of the sewing kit and a closing flap placed under the appliqué door before it is sewn in place.

Prepare the house-shaped walls by following the instructions for the Handbag House (Stiff Walls and Floor), using the pattern for the sewing kit, which is slightly smaller.

One house wall is quilted as normal, but you need to wait to sew the middle seam on the second house wall.

POCKET

Cut a piece of your chosen fabric for the pocket: this should be as wide as the house and 9cm (3½in) in height; you don't need to add a seam allowance. Iron the fabric in half to make it 4.5cm (1¾in) in height, and sew a seam approximately 5mm (¼in) down from the width edge.

Place the pocket at the bottom on the inside of the house shape, without the seam in the middle. Sew the pocket along the edge of the house shape with zigzag stitches. Then sew a quilting seam in the middle of the whole house to create two pockets, see figure A.

A

YOU WILL NEED

Various pieces of fabric
Interfacing for bags
Cotton wadding (batting)
Hook and loop fastening
Paper piecing glue or quick-
drying hobby glue

CLOSING FLAP

Fold your chosen fabric for the closing flap right sides facing, transfer the pattern for the outline of the flap and sew around. Turn right side out and iron.

Place a 2cm (¾in) long piece of hook and loop fastening on the curved end and sew in place with a cross, see figure B.

Make the appliqués, see Handbag House (Appliqués). When you have placed the appliqué parts, position the closing flap in under the door, see the photo of the sewing kit.

Sew around all the appliqués. Make sure you fasten the closing flap securely, see figure C.

Bind the edges of the house shapes, see Handbag House, Binding.

CONTENTS

Sew a heart, see Hearts (Small Hearts). It isn't necessary to sew up the reverse opening. When the heart is stuffed, press it flat again with an iron, so that it is 7–8mm (⅜in) thick.

Sew the heart in place above the pocket, see figure D.

B

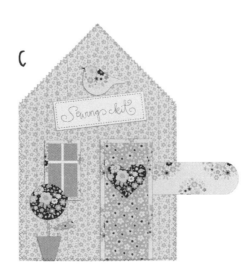

C

D

Fold the fabric for the needle holder, the scissor pocket and the scissor pocket flap in half, right sides facing. Transfer the pattern and sew around all pieces. Leave a reverse opening in the seam on the needle holder and scissor pocket.

Cut out and turn all parts right side out and iron. Fold in the seam allowance on the flap.

Sew a piece of hook and loop fastening onto the scissor holder flap in the same way as the closing flap. Sew the corresponding piece of hook and loop fastening onto the scissor pocket, see figure E. Before sewing the parts onto the house, place some scissors inside to ensure the flap fits the pocket correctly.

Press a third of the needle holder with an iron and sew it to the house along the top and bottom edges, see figure F.

Sew the two house parts together, see figure G.

Sew the corresponding piece of hook and loop fastening for the closing flap on the back of the house, ensuring that it is in the correct position for the closing loop.

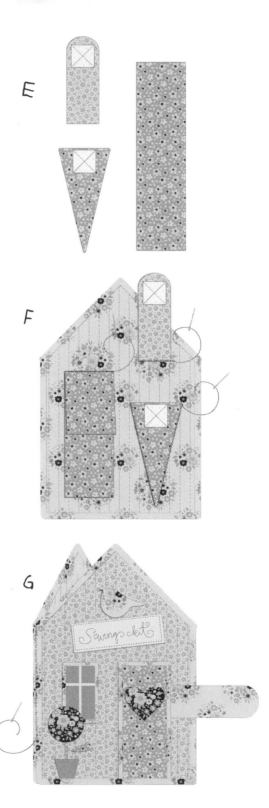

YOU WILL NEED

Fabric for the front piece, back
piece and binding
Cotton wadding (batting)
Tools for assembling, see
Patchwork and Quilting

cosy patchwork quilt

The quilt measures 46½ x 70½in (approximately 118 x 180cm).

The instructions generally describe how to make the front side of the patchwork quilt. See the section on Patchwork and Quilting for more detail about the tools, measuring units, seam allowance, wadding (batting) and back piece, quilting and binding. Note that inches are used first and centimetres are given in brackets. Seam allowances are included in the measurements for the patchwork parts.

GETTING STARTED

The quilt is made up of two different blocks each made from two different fabrics, so you get four repeated blocks, see figure B. There is also a narrow off-white border measuring 1¼in (3cm) and a border of squares measuring 2in (5cm).

Figure A shows the measurement for all the parts to be cut for the quilt, apart from the narrow border between the patchwork and edge of the square. Figure B shows how many of each part you need to cut.

The odd measurements for the Flying Geese are due to the fact that the parts are sewn together and cut in several stages. Cut the parts for the patchwork as carefully as you can, according to the measurements.

A

A 2 × 2in (5 × 5 cm)	B 2 × 3½in (5 × 8.75 cm)	A
B	C 3½ × 3½in (8.75 × 8.75 cm)	B
A	B	A

Flying Geese

D

4¼ × 4¼ in
(10.25 × 10.25 cm)

E

2⅜ × 2⅜in
(6 × 6 cm)

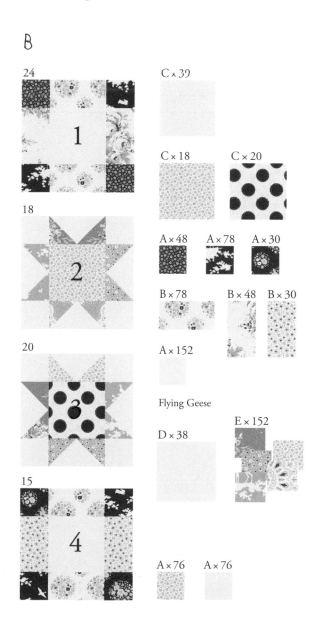

B

24 — 1

18 — 2

20 — 3

15 — 4

C × 39

C × 18   C × 20

A × 48   A × 78   A × 30

B × 78   B × 48   B × 30

A × 152

Flying Geese

D × 38   E × 152

A × 76   A × 76

59

FLYING GEESE

This makes four Flying Geese at once. The small squares are half the size of the large one.

Place two small squares right sides together with a large square, aligning them in the corners. Draw a line from corner to corner, see figure C.

Then sew in a seam allowance along each side of the line, see figure D. Cut apart along the line, see figure E. Press the triangles outwards, see figure F.

Place one small square right sides facing with one of the sewn units. Draw a line and sew in a seam allowance on each side, see figure G. Cut apart along the line and press the parts outwards. Repeat with the last small square and the other sewn unit. You will now have four identical Flying Geeses parts, see figure H.

When you have sewn all the Flying Geese pieces for the quilt, they are sewn together with a middle piece and corners into finished blocks. We have varied our pattern so that each block has different blue-patterned parts, see figure I. Also sew together the 1 block and 4 blocks.

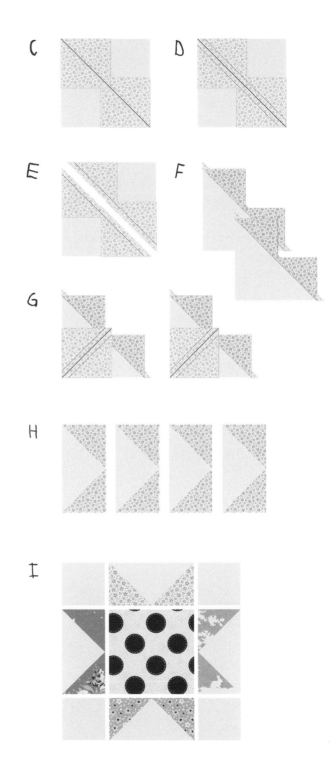

Lay out the blocks in eleven rows, each with seven blocks, see figure J. Sew the blocks together in rows, pressing the seams of alternate rows in opposite directions. Now sew the rows together and press the seams downwards.

For the narrow border cut from the off-white fabric two strips 1¼ x 42½in (3 x 108cm). Cut four strips 1¼in (3cm) x width of fabric and sew them together end to end and press seams open. From this long strip cut two strips 1¼ x 68in (3 x 173cm).

Sew the shorter off-white 1¼in (3cm) strips to the top and bottom of the quilt and press the seams outwards. Sew the longer strips to the sides of the quilt and press the seams outwards.

Then sew together the squares for the outer border and sew in place next to the narrow border. The border should finish with one blue square in each corner, see figure K.

Assemble the wadding (batting) and back piece, see Patchwork and Quilting. Finally, bind the quilt, see Binding.

CUSHION

Using the patchwork for the quilt as a starting point, you can also make matching patchwork cushions.

For the cushions use two of blocks 1 and 2 and five of block 4. The patchwork for the cushion is sewn and quilted in the same way as the quilt.

Sew a back piece for the cushion: we have sewn two parts together with a zip in the middle. Fasten the back piece and patchwork, wrong sides together, with a zigzag stitches around the edge.

Bind the cushion, see Binding.

J

K

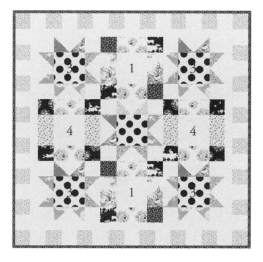

Hearts

You can find the templates in the Patterns *section.*

These lovely cushions and decorations were made using leftover fabric from the quilt.

HEART CUSHIONS

Heart cushions are sewn from fifty 2½in (6.25cm) squares, but six of the squares are lengthened to avoid ending up with too little seam allowance around the edge, see figure A. Seam allowance is included in the measurements.

Position the patchwork pieces randomly but make sure that you do not place identical pieces next to each other. The patchwork is assembled with wadding (batting) and a back piece and quilted, see Patchwork and Quilting.

Cut out a piece of fabric the same size as the patchwork and place the fabric and patchwork right sides facing. Note that the pattern has been divided up to fit on the pattern pages.

Transfer the pattern of the heart cushion and sew around it, leaving a reverse opening in the edge. Cut off the excess seam allowance and cut nicks in the seam allowance where the seam curves in. Turn the cushion right side out and stuff, then sew up the reverse opening.

A

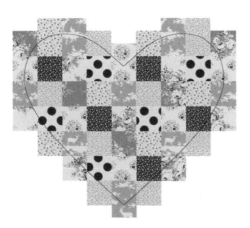

SMALL HEARTS

Press the fabric for the heart right sides facing, transfer the pattern and sew around it. Cut out the heart and cut nicks in the seam allowance where the seam curves in at the top.

Make a reverse opening through one layer of fabric, as marked on the pattern. Turn the heart right side out, press and stuff. Sew up the reverse opening. To hide the reverse opening you can cut a small piece of fabric, fold in the edges and sew it in place over the opening, like a small plaster. Preferably use a different fabric from the heart fabric for a decorative effect, see the photograph.

One heart is decorated with a variation of the flower decoration, see Decorations, where only circles are used to create a small flower.

GARLANDS

The quickest way to make a heart garland is to sew the string through the hearts with a long doll's needle. It can be difficult to thread the string through the eye of the needle; you need to make sure that the eye is big enough and the string is thin enough. Take care of the balancing point too: the thread must be as high as possible so that the hearts hang properly.

Making a doll's room

The idea behind the doll's room was Emma, my doll Meg, and the doll's doll, which meant I needed to find furniture in three different sizes. It was quite simple, thanks to a bit of rooting around in the loft. I also suggest scouring charity shops and car boot sales.

The furniture is painted in the same colours, so the beds and chairs are blue and the table is white. The colour scheme in the room is red and blue and the subject – in addition to the dolls – is the houses, in the form of the Handbag House and Sewing Kit House. Small clouds make ideal decorations on the wall.

WOODEN CLOUDS

The clouds are cut out from 2cm (¾in) thick wooden hobby board. We had help from a carpenter for the cutting, sanding and assembly, although there is no reason why you cannot do it yourself with an electric keyhole saw, sanding block, sandpaper and wood glue.

Use a pair of compasses to draw three overlapping circles of different sizes, with the largest in the middle. Then draw a line between the lowest points, so that the cloud is flat at the base, see figure A.

The clouds are made in three different sizes and painted in a slightly lighter shade of blue than the furniture. The large white dots are drawn with a pair of compasses and are outlined first with a thin brush to create an even edge. A larger brush is used to fill in the colour in the middle, see figure B.

A block of wood cut from the same hobby board is fitted to the back of the clouds to make the clouds protrude slightly from the wall.

A picture frame screw is screwed into the top of the block for hanging, see figure C. It is important to place the block and screw correctly so that the cloud hangs properly, however the screw can easily be moved if needed.

A
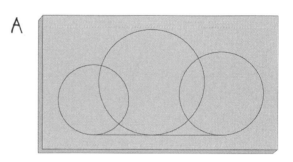

B

C

SEA and WATER

"Under the water it's interesting, exciting and sometimes a little bit fishy.
The fish can be anything from very tiny twas big as a house."

pirate

You can find the templates in the Patterns *section.*

This very charming pirate would rather go on a fishing trip than go plundering.

GETTING STARTED

Sew the doll's body, see Doll's Body, using patterned fabric instead of skin fabric, as the pirate has a patterned shirt.

Paint the hair and face, see Faces and Hair.

Sew the trousers, see Knickers and Trousers, and the hairband, see Hair Accessories.

Instead of fastening the bow to the top of the head, it is fastened at an angle on the back of the head; see the photograph of the pirate.

YOU WILL NEED

Skin fabric
Fabric for clothes
Wool stuffing
Tools for hair and face, see
Faces and Hair

YOU WILL NEED

Fabric
Flat elastic

Eye patch

You can find the templates in the Patterns *section.*

GETTING STARTED

Fold the fabric for the small eye patch in half, right sides facing. Transfer the pattern of the eye patch and mark the openings on each side. One opening should be large enough to be used to turn the eye patch right side out.

Turn the edges right side out and press the openings neatly inwards so that they follow the curves of the patch.

Cut a strip of fabric measuring approximately 32 x 2.5cm (12¾ x 1in). Iron the long sides in so they meet in the middle, then fold and iron the strip in half lengthways. It should measure approximately 7mm (¼in) wide. Sew the open sides together.

Thread the fabric strip through the two openings in the patch, so that it sticks out on each side of the patch. Use some tweezers if the fabric strip is difficult to pull through.

Fit the patch on the pirate. Both ends of the strip must be at the back of the head and the strip must be longer on one side of the patch.

Cut a length of flat elastic to fit the back section around the head, see figure A. Fasten the eye patch properly in place on the strip with a pin to stop it slipping. Sew the elastic in place between the strip ends.

Sew up the openings in the patch to fasten it to the strip, see figure B.

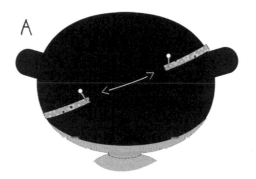

A

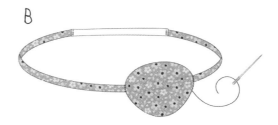

B

cute whales

You can find the templates in the Patterns *section.*

These colourful, gently curved and especially cute whales were our model's favourite. Emma was very excited on the day we photographed her with these friendly whales.

GETTING STARTED

Fold the fabric for the fins right sides facing with a piece of wadding (batting) underneath. Transfer the fin pattern and sew around it. Cut out the fins and turn them right side out with the wadding in the middle, and iron, see figure A.

Cut out two body parts and the base, according to the pattern. Note that the base is made from a different fabric from the body.

Place the two body parts, right sides facing, and sew together, leaving the flat bottom edge open, see figure B.

Using the pattern as a guide, mark where the fins are to be fastened. Use pins to fasten the fins to the edge of each side of the body, making sure the fins turn right side in.

Sew the fins in place and remove the pins, see figure C.

A

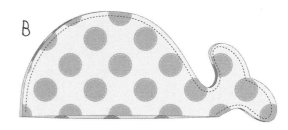

B

C

YOU WILL NEED

Fabrics
Interfacing wadding (batting)
Wool stuffing
Wooden stick
Tools for the eyes, see
Faces and Hair

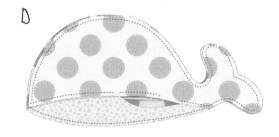

Fold the base in half and mark the middle at the front. Place the whale body right sides facing on the base and make sure that the middle at the front of the base and the body are aligned.

First sew one side, from the middle at the front backwards to the tail. Then sew the other side, allowing a reverse opening at the fin, see figure D.

Cut off the excess seam allowance around the edge and use a wooden stick to turn the whale right side out as much as possible.

Stuff the whale, tail first, using the wooden stick. Stuff the rest of the body well and sew up the reverse opening.

Add the eyes, see Faces and Hair.

small sardines

You can find the templates in the Patterns *section.*

It's easy to sew a whole shoal of sardines. They are a cute decoration to brighten up any room, not just children's bedrooms, and their simple design makes them perfect to add to keyrings.

GETTING STARTED

Cut out two strips of fabric large enough for the head and two pieces of a different fabric large enough for the body. Allow for plenty of seam allowance on all edges.

Sew the two fabrics together and press, right sides facing, so that the same fabrics face each other.

Transfer the pattern for the sardine and sew around it. Remember the reverse opening, see figure A.

Cut out then turn the sardine right side out, press and stuff. Sew up the reverse opening.

Add the eyes, see Faces and Hair.

A

YOU WILL NEED

Fabrics
Wool stuffing
Tools for the eyes, see Faces
and Hair

YOU WILL NEED

Fabric for the front piece, back piece and binding

Cotton wadding (batting)

Tools for assembling, see Patchwork and Quilting

patchwork quilt in blue

The quilt measures 51 x 75in (127.5 x 187.5cm)

A patchwork quilt in blue is perfect for a nautical-themed room. The instructions generally describe how to make the patchwork. The section on Patchwork and Quilting gives more detail about the tools, measuring units, seam allowance, wadding and back piece, quilting and binding. Note that inches are used as the primary measuring unit; centimetres are given in brackets. Seam allowances are included in the measurements for the patchwork parts.

GETTING STARTED

To make the cutting job simpler, the triangles for the border around the edge of the quilt are cut out of squares. In the cutting plan, this is part E and F.

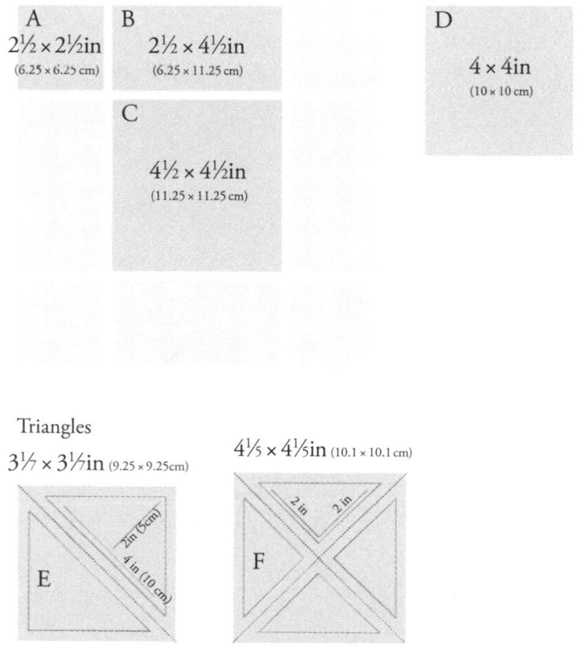

Since the A and C parts are repeated at different intervals, no blocks are made, but if you look at the illustration of the whole quilt you can get a good idea of how the parts should be assembled.

The nine different C parts are repeated as set out below. Cut out all the parts for the quilt according to the measurements in figure A; the quantity is shown in figure B.

A   Blocks

A
2½ × 2½in
(6.25 × 6.25 cm)

B
2½ × 4½in
(6.25 × 11.25 cm)

C
4½ × 4½in
(11.25 × 11.25 cm)

D
4 × 4in
(10 × 10 cm)

Triangles

3⅐ × 3⅐in (9.25 × 9.25cm)

E
2in (5cm)
4 in (10 cm)

4⅕ × 4⅕in (10.1 × 10.1 cm)

F
2 in
2 in

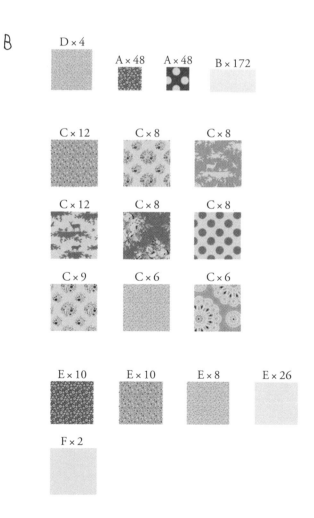

B

D × 4

A × 48   A × 48   B × 172

C × 12   C × 8   C × 8

C × 12   C × 8   C × 8

C × 9   C × 6   C × 6

E × 10   E × 10   E × 8   E × 26

F × 2

Start sewing together the patchwork, see figure C. Note that the small squares in the main area are repeated alternately. If you sew smaller blocks first based on the larger squares as shown, make sure that the small squares are not repeated in the same way in each block.

TRIANGLE BORDER

When the triangle border is sewn together, the short sides are placed facing each other, as shown in figure D.

C

Fold away from each other and sew the next triangle in place, see figures E and F. Finish on each side with the corner pieces cut out from part F.

The strips in off-white, which are part of the border, must be cut 2in (5cm) wide and 44¼in (113cm) and 68in (173cm) long respectively, although it is a good idea to cut them a little longer and then trim them when they are sewn to the border.

Sew the corner parts in place in the borders and sew the borders to the patchwork.

Read the Patchwork and Quilting section for more advice about how to assemble and quilt. Bind the quilt, see Binding.

D   E   F

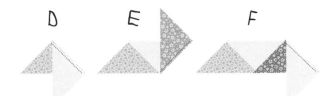

CUSHION

This is an example of how you can assemble the patchwork as a cushion with the same patchwork squares used for the quilt.

Making a sea room

The sea room was especially fun to make, and we think it looks really great. The bed has been made into a boat by fastening a sail to the edge and a complementary garland of flags has been fastened to the mast. A simple homemade wardrobe in the shape of a beach hut was designed and made by a carpenter.

BEACH HUT

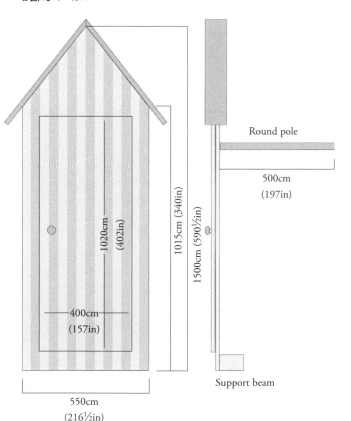

1020cm
(402in)

1015cm (340in)

1500cm (590½in)

400cm
(157in)

Round pole

500cm
(197in)

Support beam

550cm
(216½in)

BEACH HUT WARDROBE

A carpenter made the beach hut based on the drawings but with a little patience and the correct tools you can learn how to make the hut yourself.

The round pole at the back of the beach hut is fastened to the wall and there is also a beam at the bottom of the hut for support. If you want a hut that can be played in, it's a good idea to talk to a carpenter for more solid solutions.

We used wooden hobby boards, 9cm (3½in) wide planks for the roof, a round pole and a wooden knob as a door handle. You will also need a keyhole saw or similar and quality wood glue.

The carpenter made the hole for the round pole halfway into the wall using a hole saw. The pole was then glued firmly in place. It can also be fastened by a screw from the front, which is later hidden by the door when it is glued in place on the front. The pole can be fastened to the wall using a pole bracket.

FISHING ROD

Bamboo poles can be obtained from florists and garden centres.

Tie some string to one end and sew a fish to the end of the string.

SAIL

We have used various blue-patterned fabrics combined with off-white, red-spotted fabric for the flag, a wooden pole with a diameter of approximately 2.5cm (1in) and string.

The sail is sewn from 6.5cm (2½in) triangles, seam allowance included.

The patchwork for the sail is twelve pieces at the widest point and slants twenty patches up to two at the narrowest point. It's worth cutting the lowest and top patches a little longer, so you have enough seam allowance when the sail is reverse sewn.

Sew a 5cm (2in) wide strip along the long side, see figure A.

Cut a piece of fabric for the back, as big as the sail, and place the sail and fabric right sides facing. Draw the sail according to the measurements and sew around, allowing a reverse opening at the edge. Cut off the excess seam allowance, turn the sail right side out and iron.

Fold in and sew the edge in place so the off-white strip is at the back and you get a hem for the wooden pole. Try out the wooden pole before you sew to make sure the channel is the right size.

FLAG FOR THE SAIL

You can find the template for the sail's flag in the Patterns *section.*

Fold the fabric for the flag right sides facing and sew around the whole flag. Make a reverse opening through one layer of fabric, as marked on the pattern. Cut out, turn the flag right side out and press.

Fold and sew in an edge, as marked on the pattern, so that you get the right sized channel for the wooden pole, see figure B.

Fasten some string to the long end of the sail, so that it can be stretched out and fastened to the bed easily, see figure C.

FLAGS FOR THE GARLAND

A selection of blue-patterned fabrics have been used for the flag garland. The flags are sewn in the same way as the flag for the sail, but only a small channel for string is sewn in, see figure D.

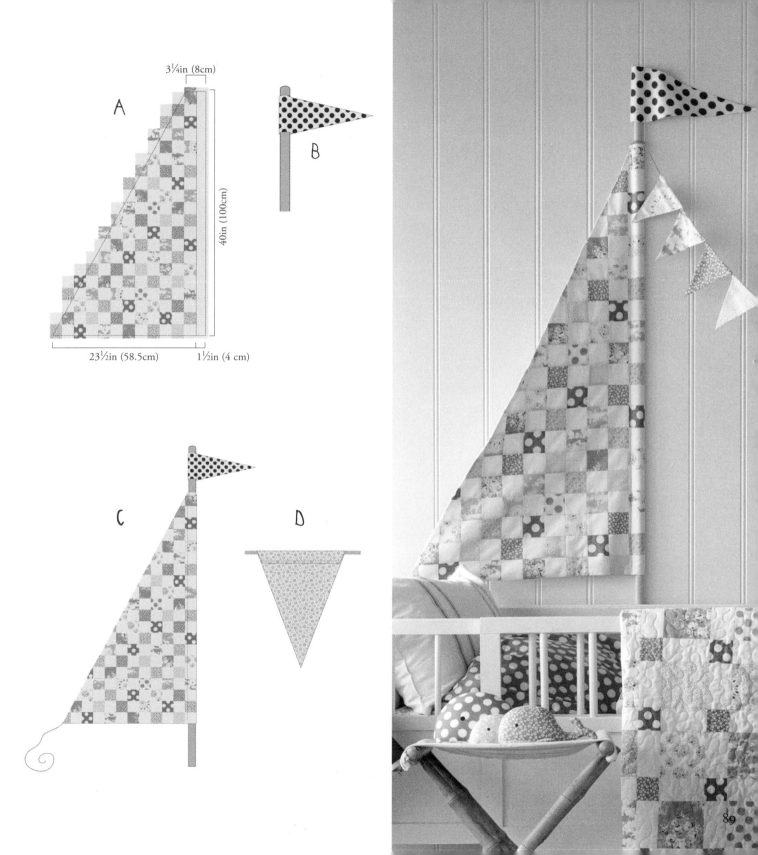

A

$3\frac{1}{4}$in (8cm)

40in (100cm)

$23\frac{1}{2}$in (58.5cm) $1\frac{1}{2}$in (4 cm)

B

C

D

EXOTIC ANIMALS

"Imagine having a room that's a jungle full of exotic animals. Animals that are so exotic that they can only be found in your room."

YOU WILL NEED

Fabrics
Iron-on interfacing
Embroidery thread
Wool stuffing
Tools for the face, see Faces
and Hair
Wooden stick for reversing

Hook monkeys

You can find the templates in the Patterns *section.*

The hook monkeys are a favourite with those of us involved in the book and we've been left with plenty of photos of these sweet creatures. They are sewn with curved arms, legs and tail so they can be hung up grasping onto things in a number of interesting ways.

GETTING STARTED

HEAD

Iron the interfacing onto a piece of skin-coloured fabric big enough for two face shapes. Transfer the pattern of the face shape onto the skin-coloured fabric twice so you have a left and right side. Pull the paper off, so only the glue remains on the fabric.

Cut out the face shapes carefully along the line, apart from the gradual curve, which must be sewn into the seam between the head shapes. Seam allowance must be included here, see figure A.

Cut out four head shapes (with seam allowance) from the fabric for the body. Note that the front head and back head are different, and make sure that you have two opposite shapes for each head part.

Mark where the face is to go (see the pattern) and iron the face shapes in place with the glue side facing the right side of the head fabric, see figure B.

Place the two head shapes on the face shapes, right sides facing, and sew up the gradual curve, see figure C.

Open out the face shapes and press. Sew a thick zigzag seam around the face shape using thread in the same colour as the face fabric, see figure D.

Sew the two shapes for the back of the head together in the same way. Place the two finished head shapes right sides facing and sew together.

Cut off the excess seam allowance and cut nicks in the seam where it curves in at the neck.

Turn the head right side out and iron. Stuff the head well and shape it until you are happy.

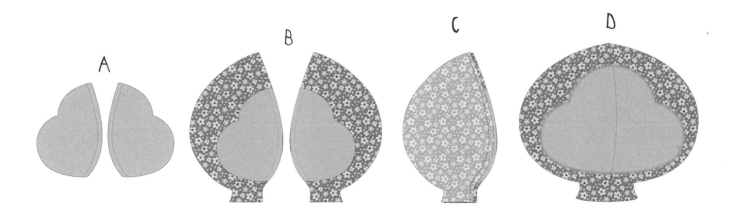

A   B   C   D

BODY

Iron the fabric for the body in half, right sides facing, and transfer the pattern for the body, two arms, two legs and a tail. Mark the openings.

Sew around the pieces, paying attention to where the openings are. Bear in mind that the two cut-ins for the base at the bottom of each side of the body must be open, although you will need to sew a small seam to hold the fabrics together on each side of the base.

Cut out all parts and cut nicks in the seam allowance where the seam curves in. Fold the openings at the base of the body in opposite ways, so the seams are against each other, and sew across the opening on each side, see figures E and F.

Turn the parts right side out, using a wooden stick to make it easier to turn the arms, legs and tail. Iron the pieces.

Stuff the body parts using the wooden stick to help you, and sew up the reverse openings.

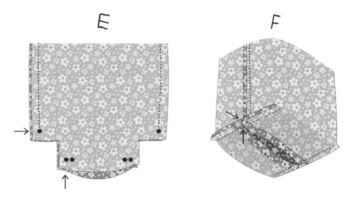

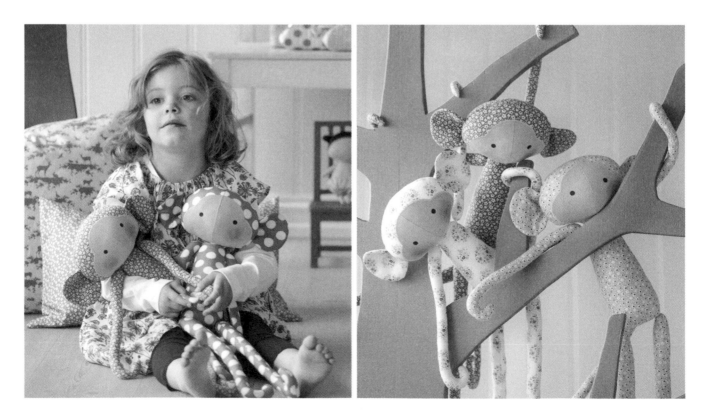

96

EARS

Fold the fabric for the ears, right sides facing, and place a piece of interfacing wadding (batting) underneath. Transfer the ears pattern and sew around the ears, see figure G. Cut out, turn right side out with the interfacing in the middle, fold the seam allowance in at the openings and iron the ears.

Fold in the seam allowance around the neck and sew the head securely onto the body.

Bend the ears slightly and fasten with pins on each side of the head before sewing them securely into place, see the photo of the monkeys for reference. Remove pins.

The arms and legs must have plenty of movement and therefore must have a small fastening point. Embroidery thread makes the fastening stronger. Sew the arms, legs and tail securely with embroidery thread, see figure H. Finish the face, see Faces and Hair.

G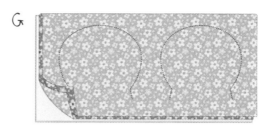

H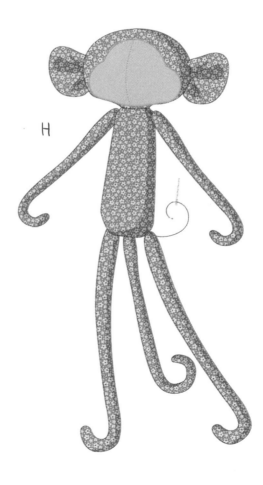

patchwork snake

You can find the templates in the Patterns *section.*

A patchwork snake can be used as many things: a cushion, a soft toy and a decoration. The pattern pages only contain the patterns for the head and tip of the tail. The rest of the body is sewn from patches of equal size.

GETTING STARTED

HEAD

Fold a piece of fabric for the tongue in half, right sides facing. Transfer the pattern, sew and cut out the tongue. Remember to cut nicks in the seam allowance where the seam curves in. Turn the tongue right side out, using the wooden stick to help you, and iron.

Transfer the pattern and cut out the two opposite shapes for the top part of the head and the two opposite shapes for the bottom part. Place both head pairs right sides together so they align along the right edge. Place the tongue into one part, as marked on the pattern, and sew the parts together, see figure A.

Iron the two sewn-together parts away from each other and place right sides together. Sew together a small section of the top of the head, fold out and iron, see figure B.

BODY

The patches for the body are cut at 8.5 x 3in (approximately 21 x 7.5cm), seam allowance included. We have used 39 patches: 20 off-white and 19 patterned.

Cut out and sew together all the patches, starting and ending with the off-white patches.

A
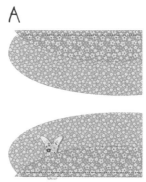

B
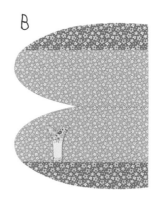

YOU WILL NEED

Fabrics
Wool stuffing
Tools for the face, see
Faces and Hair
Wooden stick for
reversing

Cut a patch that is large enough for the tip of the tail twice and sew one piece to the end of the body. Sew the head to the other end, see figure C.

Fold the whole of the snake body right sides together. Transfer the pattern of the tail onto the fabric at the opposite end of the head.

Draw a line the length of the body from the head until you get just over halfway down the body; here you need to start slanting the line to form the tail shape, see figure D.

Sew the body together along the drawn line, allowing a reverse opening in the seam. Make sure the tongue isn't in the way of the seam. Cut off the excess seam allowance around the edge, turn the snake right side out and iron.

Try not to overstuff the snake; add the stuffing in stages and check that the body can be bent easily before adding more stuffing.

Sew up the reverse opening and make the eyes, see Faces and Hair.

C   D

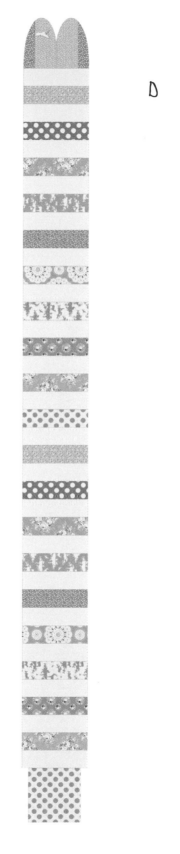

You can find the templates in the Patterns *section.*

These very talkative parrots are closely related to the common parrot, only they are smaller. Their legs are fastened to allow them to sit comfortably on the edge of a table or shelf.

GETTING STARTED

BODY

Roughly cut out two opposite beaks and opposite body shapes. Make sure that you carefully cut a seam allowance where the body and beak are sewn together. Sew the beak parts to the body parts and press the sewn-together shapes away from each other.

Place the two body parts right sides together, draw the outline of the pattern if necessary and mark the reverse opening. Sew around, see figure A.

Cut off the excess seam allowance and cut nicks in the seam allowance where the seam curves in. Turn the body right side out using the wooden stick, then iron. Stuff the body well.

A

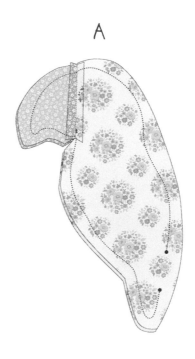

YOU WILL NEED

Fabrics
Wool stuffing
Tools for the face, see Faces and Hair
Wooden stick for reversing

WINGS AND FEATHERS

Fold the fabric for the wings, short tail feathers and long tail feathers in half and press. Place the wadding (batting) under the folded fabric.

Transfer the pattern for two wings, two short tail feathers and one long feather and sew around the parts. Cut out the parts and make reverse openings through one layer of the fabric, as marked on the pattern. Turn the parts right side out using the wooden stick, then press.

Sew the wings securely on each side by sewing on the underside of the wing without sewing through it.

Sew the two small tail feathers on each side of the tail and place the large tail feather slightly further up in the middle at the back, see figure B.

FEET

Iron the fabric for the feet, right sides facing, and transfer the pattern. Cut out the parts, remembering to cut nicks in the seam allowance where the seams curve in.

Turn the feet right side out using the wooden stick then press. Stuff the feet well using the wooden stick. Push in the seam allowance around the opening with the wooden stick and fasten the feet to the body with pins. Place the chatterbox parrot on the edge of a table and adjust the legs until it can stand by itself. Sew the legs in place and remove all pins.

Finish the face, see Faces and Hair.

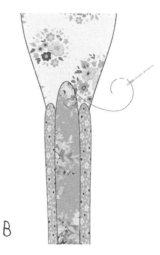

B

purses

You can find the templates in the Patterns *section.*

Small purses can be pretend exotic fruit for the jungle room. They fit 9cm (3½in) wide Tilda bag clasps.

GETTING STARTED

Cut out a piece of fabric large enough for two of each purse half and a piece of wadding (batting) in the same size.

Place the wadding under the fabric. Transfer the pattern for the purse onto the right side of the fabric, using either an air erasable pen or with faint pencil marks. Roughly quilt the purse parts on the fabric side, following the dotted lines in the pattern.

Cut out the parts, remembering to include a seam allowance. Cut out equivalent parts in the lining fabric, see figure A.

Sew the four fabric parts together at the base, see figure B.

Sew the lining parts together in the same way and place with the fabric pieces right sides facing. Sew the small curve on the top and the base of the sewn-together part, as marked with two dots on the pattern. Also sew the small V cut-in on each side, as shown in figure C.

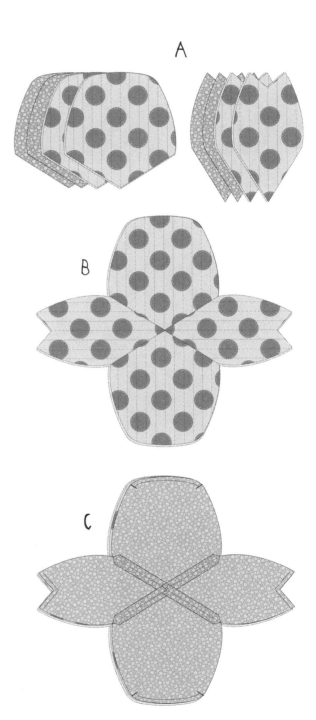

A

B

C

Take hold of the middle of the fabric piece and the middle of the lining piece and pull the fabric and lining apart. The sides that now meet, lining against lining and fabric against fabric between the sewn areas, must be sewn together. Leave a reverse opening in the lining part, see figure D.

Cut off any excess seam allowance and turn the purse right side out. Push the lining part down into the inside of the purse, see figure E.

Fasten the clasp in the normal way, by placing the curve into the clasp and sewing it in place using the holes in the clasp.

Fold the fabric for the leaves in half, right sides facing. Place wadding underneath if you want padded leaves, although it is easier to turn it right side out without wadding.

Use the pattern to draw two leaves, then sew around and cut out the leaves. Make a reverse opening through one layer of fabric, turn the leaves right side out and iron.

Sew the leaves in place on the purse, adding a button on top, see the photograph.

D

E

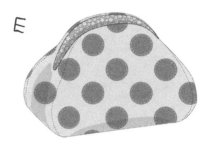

Monkey cushion

You can find the template in the Patterns *section.*

Monkeys make sweet appliqué motifs and this cheeky cushion is a cute addition to the jungle room. The cushion is appliquéd by gluing fabric around paper pieces with paper piecing glue and sewing them in place by hand.

GETTING STARTED

Print out the parts for the appliqué on photocopier paper. Cut out the paper pieces and cut out the fabric parts with approximately 1cm (⅜in) seam allowance around the edge.

Glue the edges of the fabric parts over the edges of the paper pieces, see figure A.

Cut out a background for the appliqué measuring 12 x 20in (30 x 50cm).

Position the appliqué shapes on the background, see figure B. The shapes can vary in size and any excess can be cut off at the edges.

Secure the appliqué shapes to the background with a little paper piecing glue, or pin and sew them in place. Only sew on the fabric edge; avoid sewing through the paper as this has to be removed later. Use small invisible stitches on the front. Sew the face in place on the head fabric.

YOU WILL NEED

Fabrics
Printout of the pattern
Paper piecing glue
Interfacing wadding (batting)
Tools for the face, see Faces and Hair

A

When all parts have been sewn securely in place, snip the background fabric at the back of the appliquéd parts and jiggle the paper pieces out. The glue will now be dry and brittle and the paper should be easy to remove. If the paper breaks and is difficult to get out, use tweezers to help.

First take out the paper from the head then snip the fabric at the back of the head and pull out the paper from the face.

Any loose edges at the back can be glued down with the appliqué using a little paper piecing glue, so they stay in place when the cushion is padded and quilted.

The cushion is assembled with wadding (batting) and a back piece, and quilted around the appliqué pieces. See the section on Patchwork and Quilting for more advice about assembling and quilting.

We've sewn a cushion back piece from two pieces of fabric sewn together with a zip in the middle and then we reverse-sewn the cushion. Alternatively, you can sew the parts wrong sides facing with a zigzag seam around the edge, and then bind, see Binding.

Make the monkey's face, see Faces and Hair.

B

patchwork snake quilt

The quilt measures 48 x 71in (120 x 177.5cm)

This quilt is made from patchwork snake skin; let's hope they weren't relatives of the Patchwork Snake! The instructions describe how to make the patchwork. See the section on Patchwork and Quilting for more detail about the tools, measuring units, seam allowance, wadding and back piece, quilting and binding. Note that inches are used as the primary measuring unit; centimetres are given in brackets. Seam allowances are included in the measurements for the patchwork parts.

GETTING STARTED

The quilt is mainly sewn from two blocks: A and B, which are repeated alternately to make patchwork strips. There are strips of off-white fabric between the patchwork strips. At each end, there is a triangle border the same size as the Patchwork Quilt in Blue.

As explained for the Patchwork Quilt in Blue, it is easier to cut the triangles out from squares. Figure A illustrates the size of square you will need to cut to make triangles (E). You need 12 patterned and 11 off-white squares, which are cut as shown, see figure A. You will also need four corners, which are made by dividing one of the squares into four, as shown (F).

You will need 16 of each for blocks A and B. All pieces must be 5½in (14cm) in height. So you end up with 16 A blocks and 16 B blocks.

Start by cutting out all the pieces for the patchwork.

You will also need the following strips of off-white fabric:

Two strips measuring 1½ x 48½in (3.75 x 123cm)

Two strips measuring 2½ x 48½in (6.25 x 123cm)

Seven strips measuring 3¼ x 48½in (8 x 123cm)

A Triangles
12 patterned (24 triangles)
11 off white (22 triangles)
1 (4 corner pieces)

3½ x 3½in (9.25 x 9.25cm)   4 x 4in (10 x 10.cm)

E   F

B   16 of each

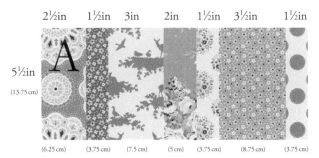

2½in	1½in	3in	2in	1½in	3½in	1½in

5½in (13.75 cm)   A

(6.25 cm) (3.75 cm) (7.5 cm) (5 cm) (3.75 cm) (8.75 cm) (3.75 cm)

16 of each

2½in	1½in	3in	2in	1½in	3½in	1½in

5½in (13.75 cm)   B

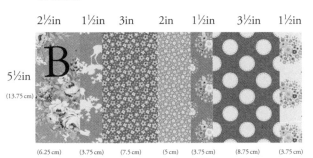

(6.25 cm) (3.75 cm) (7.5 cm) (5 cm) (3.75 cm) (8.75 cm) (3.75 cm)

YOU WILL NEED

Fabrics for the patchwork
Fabrics for the back piece
Cotton quilting wadding
(batting)
Tools for assembling, see
Patchwork and Quilting

Sew the A and B blocks together, as shown in figure B, and then sew the blocks together in strips of four. Alternate strips start with an A block and a B block, see figure C.

Sew the triangle borders, see Patchwork Quilt in Blue. Note that the two borders are identical, although the bottom one is upside down. Sew the quilt parts together, as shown in figure C.

Read the Patchwork and Quilting section for more advice about how to assemble and quilt. Bind the quilt, see Binding.

C

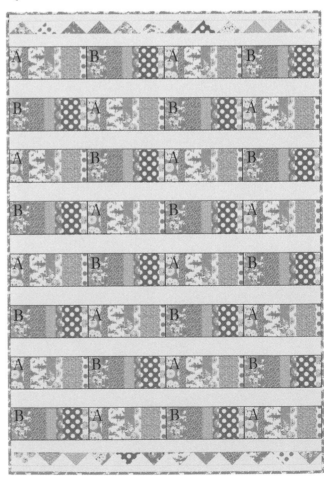

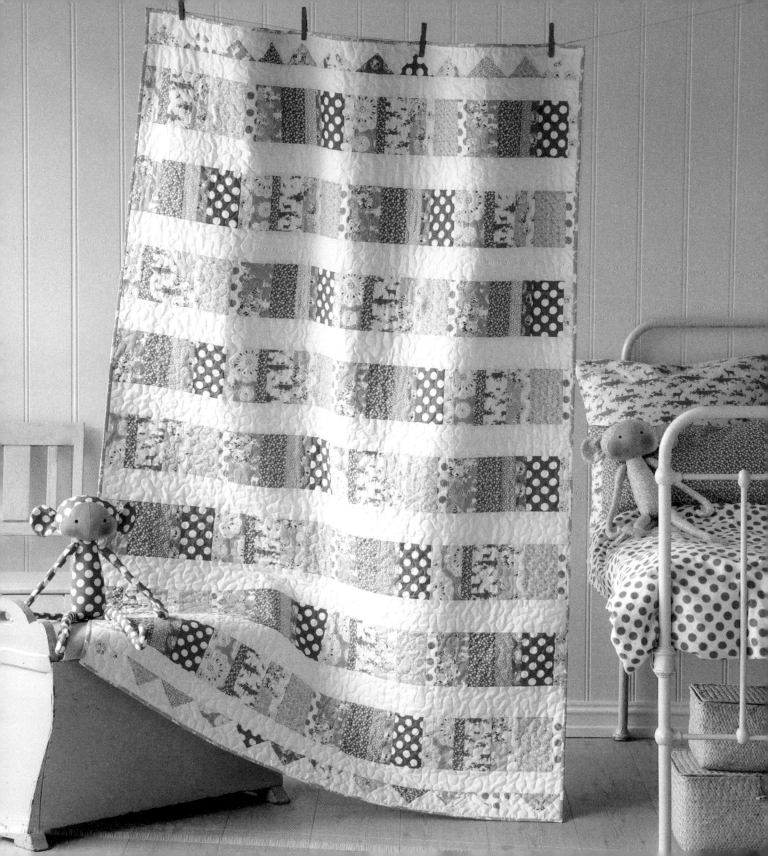

Making the jungle room

In the jungle room it's important to have furniture that the animals can enjoy climbing around on. We chose an old iron bed, which we shortened and painted in a light colour; its bars are ideal for monkeys to hang from and snakes to coil around. Also, old iron beds are magnetic, which is always fun in a child's room.

The tree is the most important element in the room, perfect for housing exotic animals. Hook monkeys will love to hang from the trailing rope, attached to the ceiling like a vine. In front of the tree is an inviting reading corner with comfy cushions. We've used a three-tier flower box, suitable for storing tales about jungle adventures and exotic animals.

JUNGLE TREE

This project requires some experience and woodworking tools.

We must emphasise that only hook monkeys and other sewn animals should climb on the tree; it is not suitable for children.

We made the tree by printing it out from the illustration, see figure A, where each square represents 30 x 30cm (12 x 12in) with a width of two thick hobby boards. We put the boards next to each other, painted and drew the squares, so the divide between the boards was in the middle of the network of squares. We then drew the tree according to our printout.

The two halves of the tree were cut out by a carpenter and glued together to make a whole tree. The edges were smoothed off with sandpaper.

To stop the tree from toppling over, we attached two supporting blocks and a board at the bottom, see figure B.

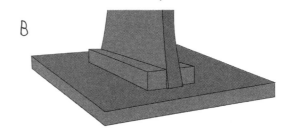

patterns

All patterns are full size.

Note: a seam allowance must be added to all pieces in the pattern, unless described otherwise in the instructions.

ES: extra seam allowance. This indicates areas where it is especially important to allow for a wider seam allowance.

Dotted line: marks openings and indicates the division between two fabrics or a pattern join.

Width edge: means that the pattern must be reversed on the other side of the width edge.

A–B: If a pattern is too large to fit on the page and has to be divided up, A–B points mark where a pattern part has to be put together with another so that points A and B lie next to each other.

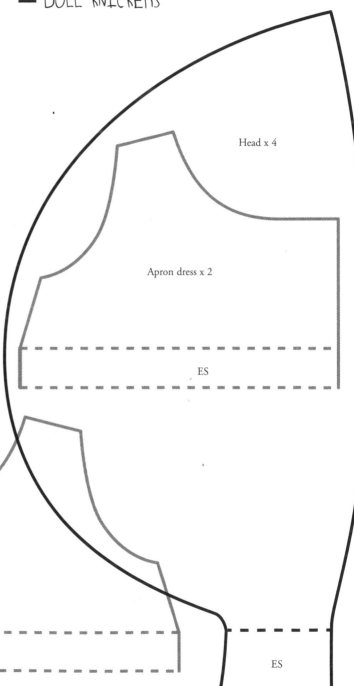

Head x 4

Apron dress x 2

ES

Apron dress x 2

ES

ES

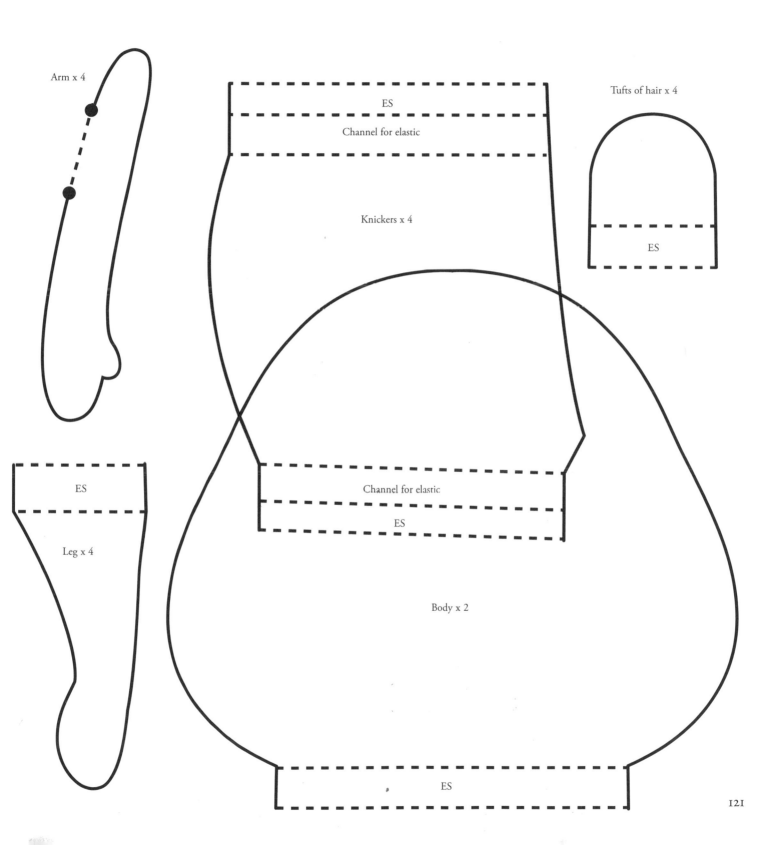

Arm x 4

ES

Channel for elastic

Tufts of hair x 4

Knickers x 4

ES

Channel for elastic

ES

ES

Leg x 4

Body x 2

ES

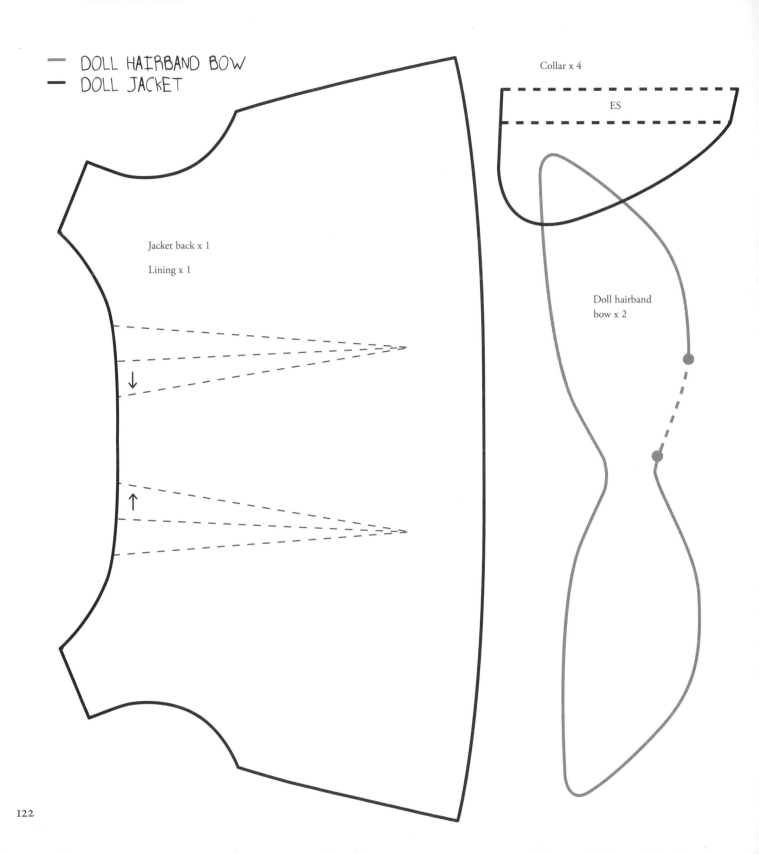

DOLL HAIRBAND BOW
DOLL JACKET

Jacket back x 1

Lining x 1

Collar x 4

ES

Doll hairband
bow x 2

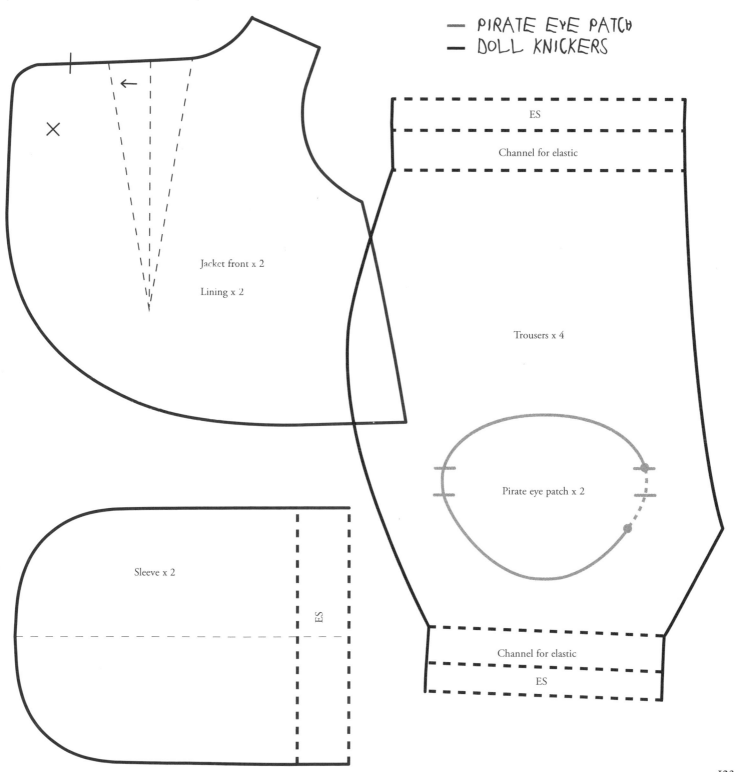

PIRATE EYE PATCH
DOLL KNICKERS

ES

Channel for elastic

Jacket front x 2

Lining x 2

Trousers x 4

Sleeve x 2

ES

Pirate eye patch x 2

Channel for elastic

ES

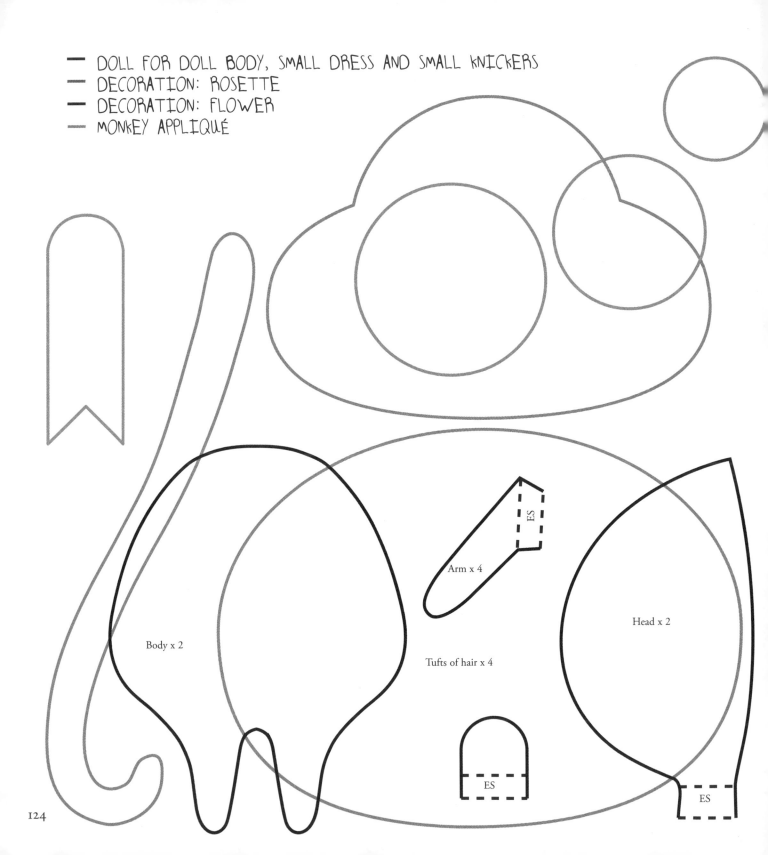

— DOLL FOR DOLL BODY, SMALL DRESS AND SMALL KNICKERS
— DECORATION: ROSETTE
— DECORATION: FLOWER
— MONKEY APPLIQUÉ

Body x 2

Arm x 4

ES

Tufts of hair x 4

Head x 2

ES

ES

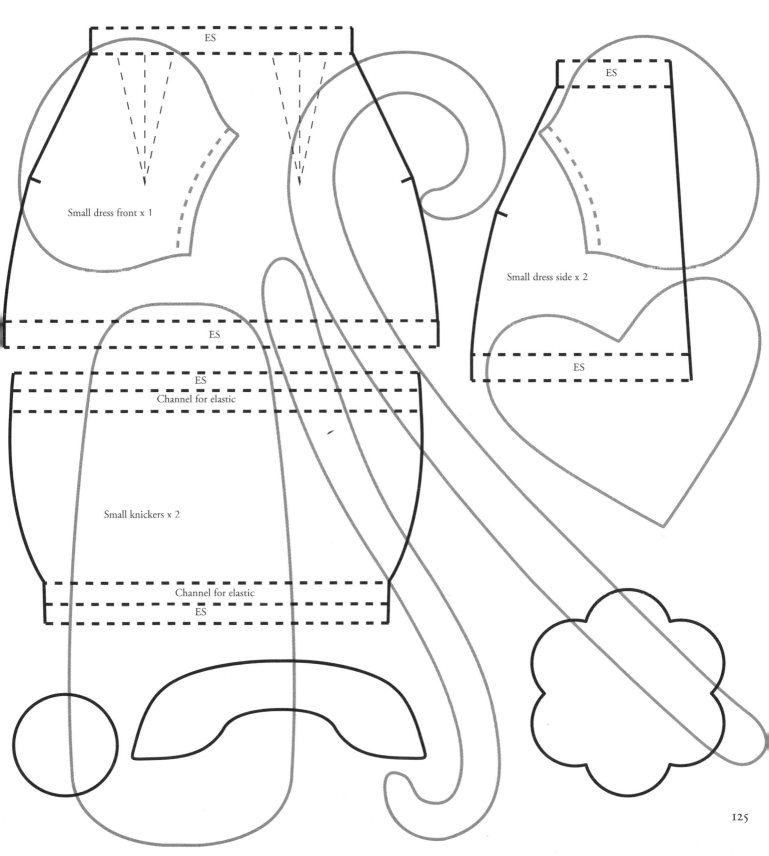

ES

Small dress front x 1

ES

Small dress side x 2

ES

ES

Channel for elastic

Small knickers x 2

Channel for elastic

ES

125

Wall interfacing x 2
Wadding (batting) x 2
Fabric x 2

— HANDBAG HOUSE
— SMALL SARDINE
— FLAG FOR GARLAND

My House

Small sardine x 2

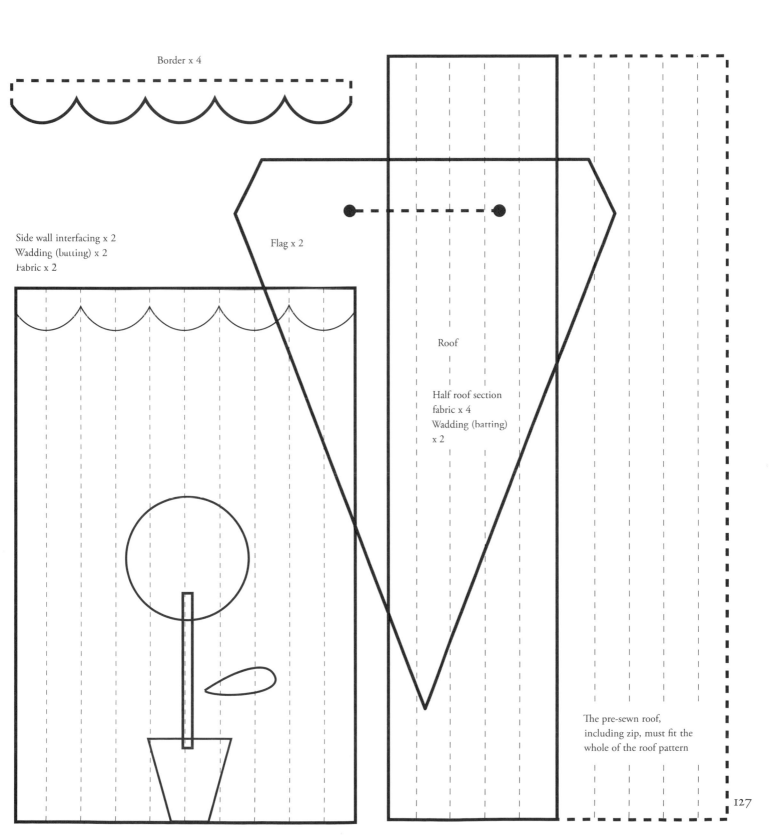

Border x 4

Side wall interfacing x 2
Wadding (batting) x 2
Fabric x 2

Flag x 2

Roof

Half roof section
fabric x 4
Wadding (batting)
x 2

The pre-sewn roof,
including zip, must fit the
whole of the roof pattern

127

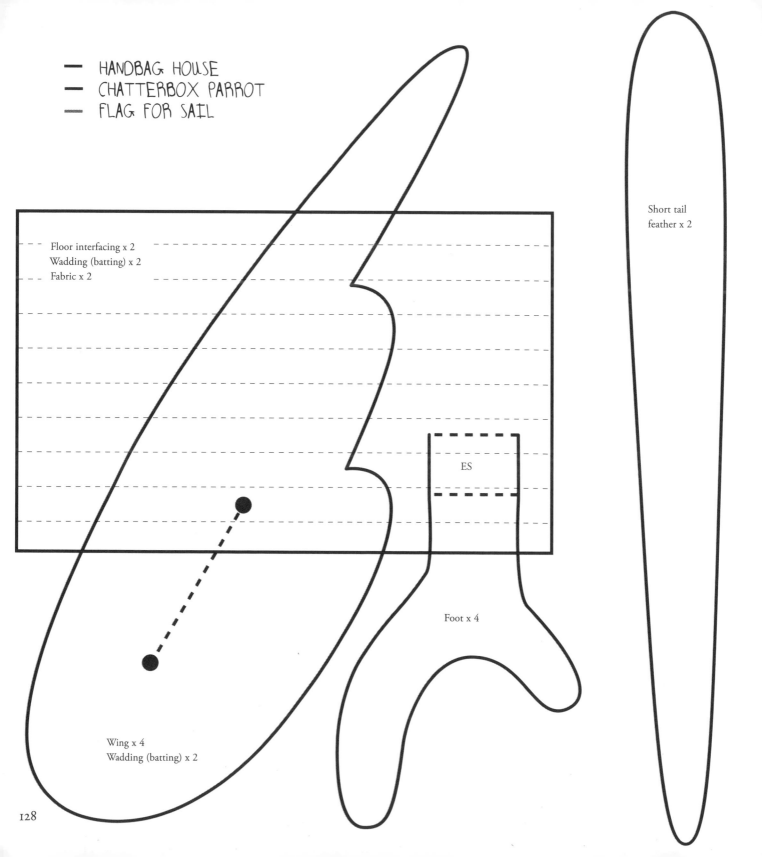

- — HANDBAG HOUSE
- — CHATTERBOX PARROT
- — FLAG FOR SAIL

Floor interfacing x 2
Wadding (batting) x 2
Fabric x 2

ES

Foot x 4

Wing x 4
Wadding (batting) x 2

Short tail
feather x 2

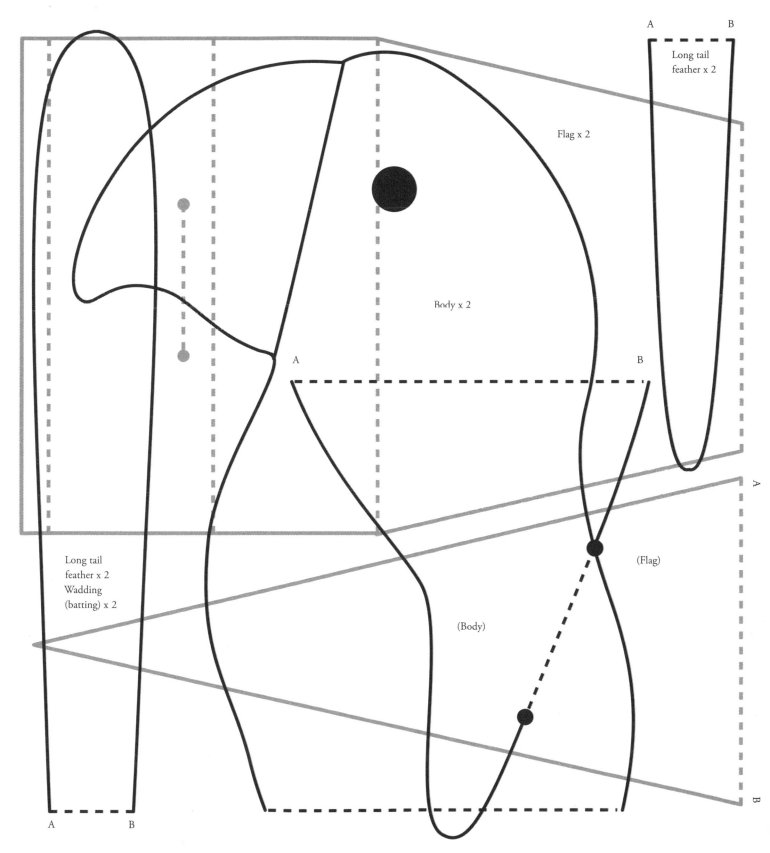

Long tail
feather x 2

A   B

Flag x 2

Body x 2

A   B

Long tail
feather x 2
Wadding
(batting) x 2

(Flag)

(Body)

A

B

A   B

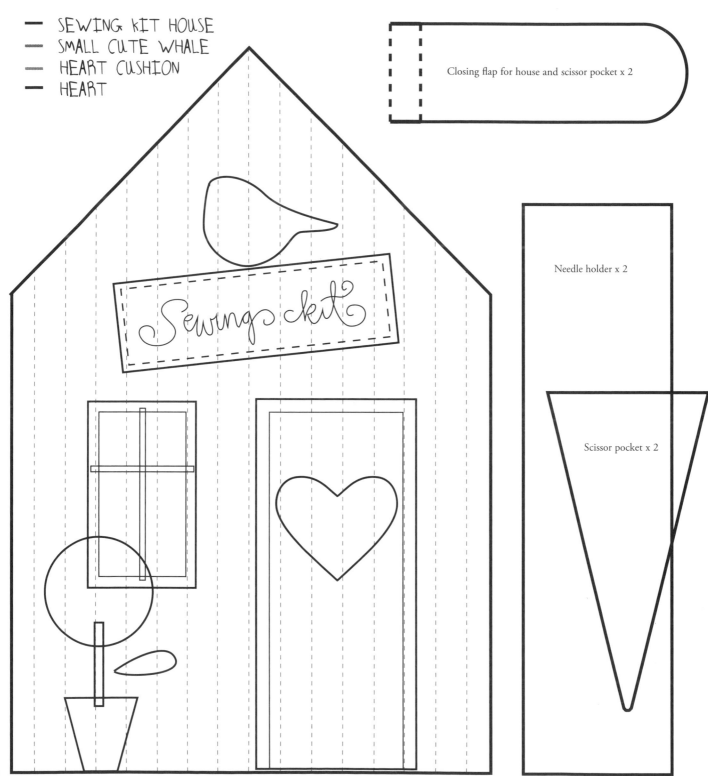

SEWING KIT HOUSE
SMALL CUTE WHALE
HEART CUSHION
HEART

Sewing kit

Closing flap for house and scissor pocket x 2

Needle holder x 2

Scissor pocket x 2

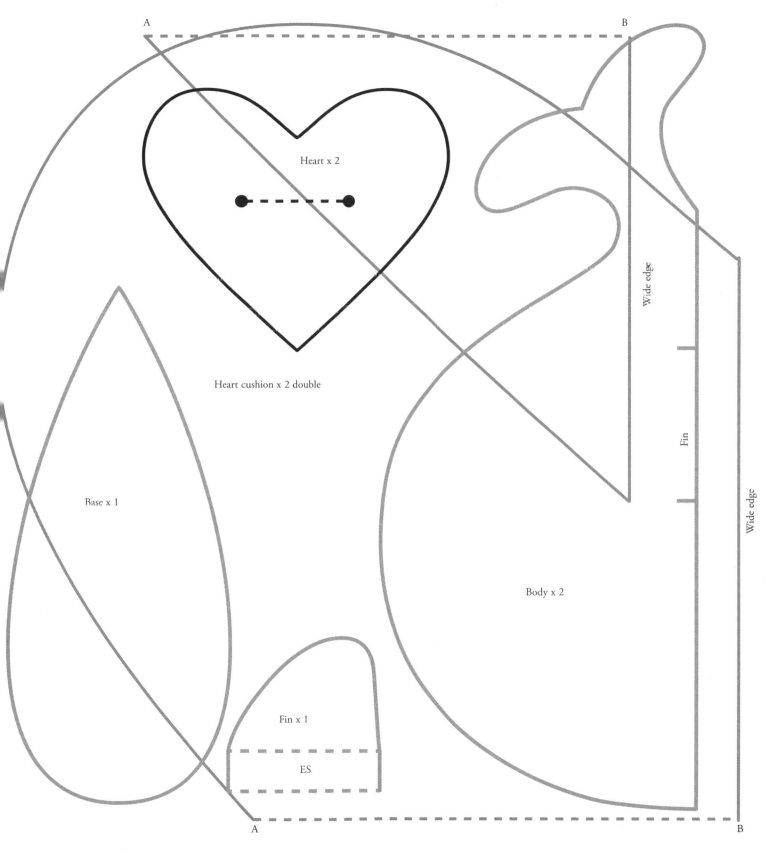

A

B

Heart x 2

Heart cushion x 2 double

Wide edge

Fin

Wide edge

Base x 1

Body x 2

Fin x 1

ES

A

B

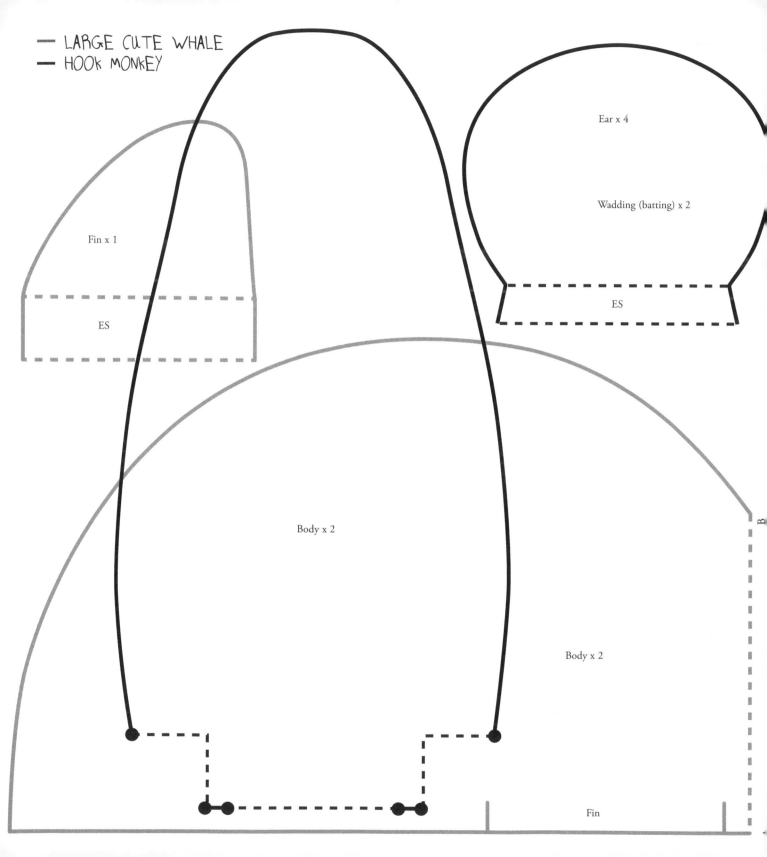

LARGE CUTE WHALE
HOOK MONKEY

Fin x 1

ES

Ear x 4

Wadding (batting) x 2

ES

Body x 2

Body x 2

B

Fin

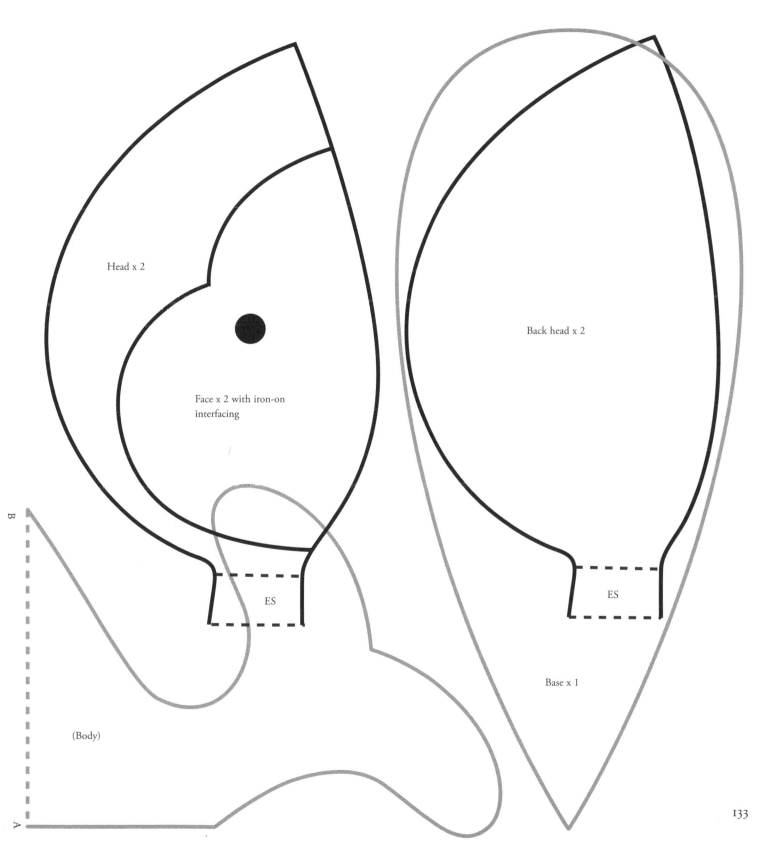

Head x 2

Face x 2 with iron-on
interfacing

Back head x 2

B

ES

ES

Base x 1

(Body)

A

133

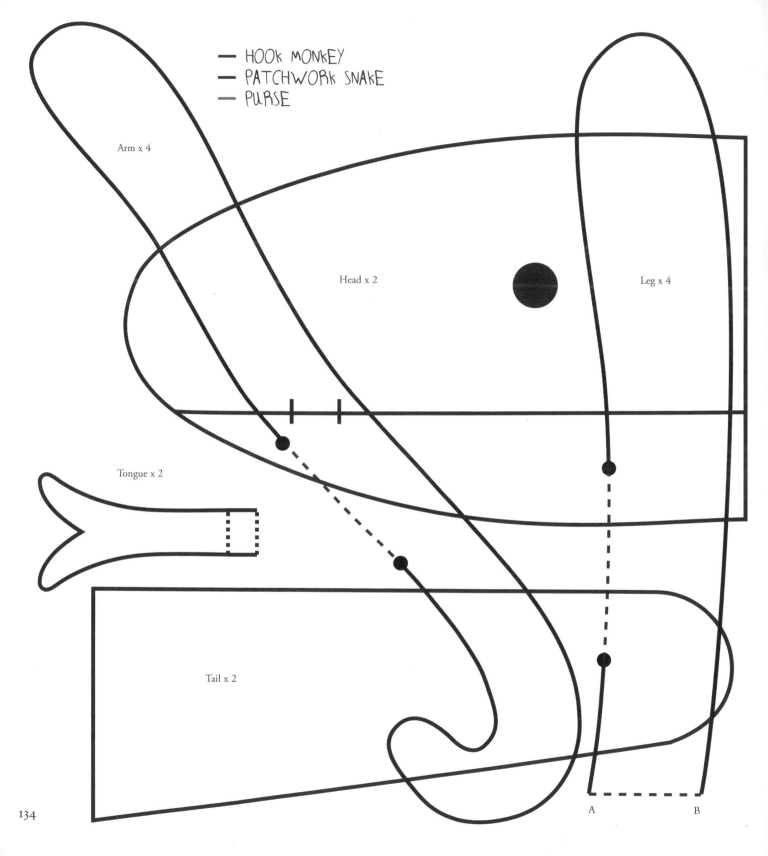

HOOK MONKEY
PATCHWORK SNAKE
PURSE

Arm x 4

Head x 2

Leg x 4

Tongue x 2

Tail x 2

A   B

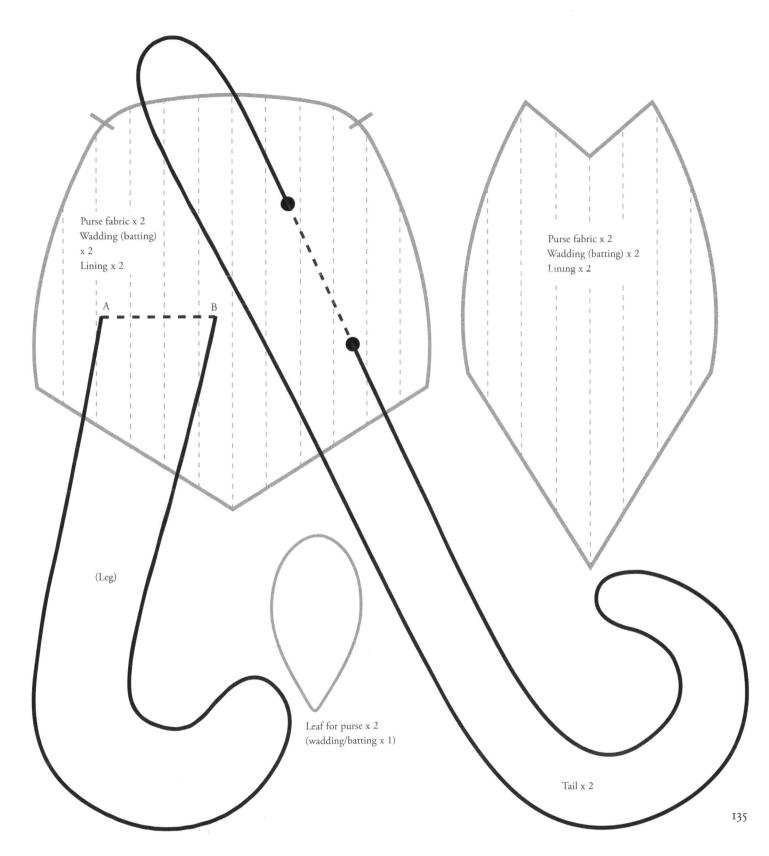

Purse fabric x 2
Wadding (batting) x 2
Lining x 2

A   B

Purse fabric x 2
Wadding (batting) x 2
Lining x 2

(Leg)

Leaf for purse x 2
(wadding/batting x 1)

Tail x 2

Suppliers

UK

Stitch Craft Create
Brunel House, Forde Close,
Newton Abbot, Devon TQ12 4PU
www.stitchcraftcreate.co.uk

Panduro Hobby
Westway House,
Transport Avenue,
Brentford, Middlesex TW8 9HF
Tel: 020 8566 1680
trade@panduro.co.uk
www.pandurohobby.co.uk

Coast and Country
Crafts & Quilts
Cornish Garden Nurseries,
Barras Moor, Perranarworthal,
Nr Truro Cornwall, TR3 7PE
www.coastandcountrycrafts.co.uk

Fred Aldous Ltd.
37 Lever Street,
Manchester, M1 1LW
www.fredaldous.co.uk

The Fat Quarters
5 Choprell Road,
Blackhall Mill,
Newcastle, NE17 7TN
www.thefatquarters.co.uk

The Sewing Bee
52 Hillfoot Street,
Dunoon, Argyll, PA23 7DT
www.thesewingbee.co.uk

Threads and Patches
48 Aylesbury Street,
Fenny Stratford, Bletchley, Milton
Keynes, MK2 2BU
www.threadsandpatches.co.uk

Puddlecrafts
3 Milltown Lodge,
Sandpit, Termonfeckin,
County Louth,
Ireland
Tel: 00353 89 439 2333
www.puddlecrafts.co.uk

Crumbly Cottage
Online shop
www.crumblycottage.com

EUROPE

Panduro Hobby
SE-205 14 Malmo, Sweden
www.pandurohobby.co.uk

Panduro Hobby (France)
BP 500, 74305 Cluses Cedex,
France
www.tildafrance.com

NORTH AMERICA

Coats and Clark USA
PO Box 12229,
Greenville, SC29612-0229
www.coatsandclark.com

Connecting Threads
13118 NE 4th Street,
Vancouver, WA 9884
www.connectingthreads.com

Hamels Fabrics
5843 Lickman Road,
Chilliwack, British Columbia,
V2R 4B5
www.hamelsfabrics.com

Keepsake Quilting
Box 1618 Center Harbor,
NH 03226
www.keepsakequilting.com

The Craft Connection
21055 Front Street
PO Box 1088
Onley, VA 23418
www.craftconn.com

Index

33614059678531